TWELFTH NIGHT

NOTES

including
- *Life of Shakespeare*
- *Brief Synopsis of the Play*
- *List of Characters*
- *Summaries and Commentaries*
- *Character Analyses*
- *Questions for Review*
- *Selected Bibliography*

by
J. L. Roberts, Ph.D.
Professor of English
University of Nebraska

Cliffs Notes
INCORPORATED
LINCOLN, NEBRASKA 68501

Editor

Gary Carey, M.A.
University of Colorado

Consulting Editor

James L. Roberts, Ph.D.
Department of English
University of Nebraska

ISBN 0-8220-0094-6
© Copyright 1982
by
C. K. Hillegass
All Rights Reserved
Printed in U.S.A.

1992 Printing

Cliffs Notes, Inc.   Lincoln, Nebraska

CONTENTS

TWELFTH NIGHT NOTES

LIFE OF SHAKESPEARE

Many books have assembled facts, reasonable suppositions, traditions, and speculations concerning the life and career of William Shakespeare. Taken as a whole, these materials give a rather comprehensive picture of England's foremost dramatic poet. Tradition and sober supposition are not necessarily false because they lack proved bases for their existence. It is important, however, that persons interested in Shakespeare should distinguish between *facts* and *beliefs* about his life.

From one point of view, modern scholars are fortunate to know as much as they do about a man of middle-class origin who left a small English country town and embarked on a professional career in sixteenth-century London. From another point of view, they know surprisingly little about the writer who has continued to influence the English language and its drama and poetry for more than three hundred years. Sparse and scattered as these facts of his life are, they are sufficient to prove that a man from Stratford by the name of William Shakespeare wrote the major portion of the thirty-seven plays which scholars ascribe to him. The concise review which follows will concern itself with some of these records.

No one knows the exact date of William Shakespeare's birth. His baptism occurred on Wednesday, April 26, 1564. His father was John Shakespeare, tanner, glover, dealer in grain, and town official of Stratford; his mother, Mary, was the daughter of Robert Arden, a prosperous gentleman-farmer. The Shakespeares lived on Henley Street.

Under a bond dated November 28, 1582, William Shakespeare and Anne Hathaway entered into a marriage contract. The baptism of their eldest child, Susanna, took place in Stratford in May, 1583. One year and nine months later their twins, Hamnet and Judith, were christened in the same church. The parents named them for the poet's friends Hamnet and Judith Sadler.

Early in 1596, William Shakespeare, in his father's name, applied to the College of Heralds for a coat of arms. Although positive proof is lacking, there is reason to believe that the Heralds granted this request, for in 1599 Shakespeare again made application for the right to quarter his coat of arms with that of his mother. Entitled to her father's coat of arms, Mary had lost this privilege when she married John Shakespeare before he held the official status of gentleman.

In May of 1597, Shakespeare purchased New Place, the outstanding residential property in Stratford at that time. Since John Shakespeare had suffered financial reverses prior to this date, William must have achieved success for himself.

Court records show that in 1601 or 1602, William Shakespeare began rooming in the household of Christopher Mountjoy in London. Subsequent disputes between Shakespeare's landlord, Mountjoy, and his son-in-law, Stephen Belott, over Stephen's wedding settlement led to a series of legal actions, and in 1612 the court scribe recorded Shakespeare's deposition of testimony relating to the case.

In July, 1605, William Shakespeare paid four hundred and forty pounds for the lease of a large portion of the tithes on certain real estate in and near Stratford. This was an arrangement whereby Shakespeare purchased half the annual tithes, or taxes, on certain agricultural products from sections of land in and near Stratford. In addition to receiving approximately ten percent income on his investment, he almost doubled his capital. This was possibly the most important and successful investment of his lifetime, and it paid a steady income for many years.

Shakespeare is next mentioned when John Combe, a resident of Stratford, died on July 12, 1614. To his friend, Combe bequeathed the sum of five pounds. These records and similar ones are important, not because of their economic significance but because they prove the existence of a William Shakespeare in Stratford and in London during this period.

On March 25, 1616, William Shakespeare revised his last will and testament. He died on April 23 of the same year. His body lies within the chancel and before the altar of the Stratford church. A rather wry inscription is carved upon his tombstone:

Good Friend, for Jesus' sake, forbear
To dig the dust enclosed here;
Blest be the man that spares these stones
And curst be he that moves my bones.

The last direct descendant of William Shakespeare was his grand-daughter, Elizabeth Hall, who died in 1670.

These are the most outstanding facts about Shakespeare the man, as apart from those about the dramatist and poet. Such pieces of information, scattered from 1564 through 1616, declare the existence of such a person, not as a writer or actor, but as a private citizen. It is illogical to think that anyone would or could have fabricated these details for the purpose of deceiving later generations.

In similar fashion, the evidence establishing William Shakespeare as the foremost playwright of his day is positive and persuasive. Robert Greene's *Groatsworth of Wit*, in which he attacked Shakespeare, a mere actor, for presuming to write plays in competition with Greene and his fellow playwrights, was entered in the *Stationers' Register* on September 20, 1592. In 1594 Shakespeare acted before Queen Elizabeth, and in 1594 and 1595 his name appeared as one of the shareholders of the Lord Chamberlain's Company. Francis Meres in his *Palladis Tamia* (1598) called Shakespeare "mellifluous and hony-tongued" and compared his comedies and tragedies with those of Plautus and Seneca in excellence.

Shakespeare's continued association with Burbage's company is equally definite. His name appears as one of the owners of the Globe in 1599. On May 19, 1603, he and his fellow actors received a patent from James I designating them as the King's Men and making them Grooms of the Chamber. Late in 1608 or early in 1609, Shakespeare and his colleagues purchased the Blackfriars Theatre and began using it as their winter location when weather made production at the Globe inconvenient.

Other specific allusions to Shakespeare, to his acting and his writing, occur in numerous places. Put together, they form irrefutable testimony that William Shakespeare of Stratford and London was the leader among Elizabethan playwrights.

One of the most impressive of all proofs of Shakespeare's authorship of his plays is the First Folio of 1623, with the dedicatory verse which appeared in it. John Heminge and Henry Condell, members of Shakespeare's own company, stated that they collected and issued the plays as a memorial to their fellow actor. Many contemporary poets contributed eulogies to Shakespeare; one of the best known of these poems is by Ben Jonson, a fellow actor and, later, a friendly rival. Jonson also criticized Shakespeare's dramatic work in *Timber: or, Discoveries* (1641).

Certainly there are many things about Shakespeare's genius and career which the most diligent scholars do not know and cannot explain, but the facts which do exist are sufficient to establish Shakespeare's identity as a man and his authorship of the thirty-seven plays which reputable critics acknowledge to be his.

BRIEF SYNOPSIS OF THE PLAY

Various critics divide this Comedy into various types of plots and/or subplots. Regardless of the exact number of plots and sub-plots, however, the main thing is that they are all woven together with immense skill to ultimately compose a single pattern or tapestry. There is, first, the group centering around the ducal nobil-ity of Illyria: this group consists of Duke Orsino and his attendants, who open the play, and the Countess Olivia, who is the main topic of discussion of the opening scene. Then there is the group of ship-wrecked personages centering on Viola and Sebastian, the twins, and their friends, Viola's sea captain who fades from the action, and, more important, Antonio, who plays a significant role later in the Comedy. Both Viola and Sebastian are, of course, later absorbed into the nobility of Illyria. Then there is the merry group of pranksters, gullers, and tricksters, led by Sir Toby Belch and Maria; this group also includes Sir Andrew Aguecheek (who is included because his in-come supports the other members of this group), Fabian, and Feste, the Clown. Through Feste, all of the groups are connected by his free movement from one group to another as he is equally at home sing-ing for Duke Orsino, or proving Lady Olivia to be a fool for so ex-cessively mourning for her brother, or in planning a trick with Sir Toby. Then outside of all of these groups stands Malvolio, Lady Olivia's puritanical steward. His colossal vanity and egotism get be-tween him and everything that he sees and does. Thus, he has already gotten on the wrong side of Maria, Feste, and Sir Toby, and the plot involving their determination to take their revenge upon him provides the best humor of the play.

Malvolio is socially and sexually ambitious; Maria realizes this and writes a letter purporting to come from the Countess Olivia, making Malvolio believe that his lady is in love with him and wishes to marry him; the letter also asks him to be firm and obstinate with her uncle, Sir Toby, to be arrogant to the other servants, and to dress in yellow stockings and go cross-gartered, and to smile all the time when he is near her. Malvolio finds the letter on the garden path and falls for the trick as he is watched gleefully by the group led by Maria and Sir Toby.

Viola disguises herself as a boy in order to protect herself and to obtain employment by Duke Orsino and quickly finds her way (as Cesario, the youth) into his favor; she is then sent to woo the Countess Olivia, much against Viola's will, for she has fallen in love with Count Orsino herself. Countess Olivia, who cannot love Duke Orsino, falls immediately in love with the messenger, Cesario, thus creating an amusing triangle which produces several complications. The arrival of Viola's twin brother, Sebastian (previously presumed drowned), sorts everything out matrimonially. Sebastian marries Olivia, Orsino marries Viola, and Sir Toby marries Maria for having played such an excellent trick on Malvolio.

This is one of Shakespeare's most popular, lightest and most musical of all his comedies, and its staging continues to delight audiences all over the world.

LIST OF CHARACTERS

Orsino

The Duke of Illyria and its ruler. At the opening of the Comedy, he is desperately in love with Lady Olivia, who spurns his romantic overtures in spite of the fact that he is a perfect and ideal gentleman.

Viola/Cesario

After being shipwrecked, she disguises herself as a young boy, takes the name of Cesario, and attains a position in Duke Orsino's household because of her wit and charm. As a boy, she is then used as an emissary from the Duke to court Lady Olivia. Her twin brother, Sebastian, looks exactly like her.

Lady Olivia

She is a rich countess who, at first, plans to mourn her brother's recent death for seven years, but when she meets the emissary from Duke Orsino (Viola disguised as a boy), she immediately falls in love with the youth.

Sebastian

The twin brother to Viola who is mistaken for Cesario when he (Sebastian) arrives in town. He meets Olivia and enters immediately into a marriage with her.

Antonio

A sea captain who aids and protects Sebastian; his pleas for help are ignored by Viola, who in her disguise looks exactly like her twin brother.

Sir Toby Belch

Lady Olivia's uncle who lives with her and who is given to constant drinking bouts; he delights in playing tricks on others.

Sir Andrew Aguecheek

A skinny knight who is encouraged by Sir Toby to continue courting Lady Olivia because as long as he courts Lady Olivia, Sir Toby can gull him out of enough money to continue the nightly drinking bouts.

Malvolio

Lady Olivia's steward who also has fantasies that Lady Olivia might someday marry him. He is opposed to Sir Toby's drinking bouts, and, thus, he becomes the object of one of Sir Toby's elaborate tricks.

Maria

Lady Olivia's waiting woman; she is clever and arranges a superlative trick to be played on Malvolio.

Feste

A Clown, or "jester," in the employ of Lady Olivia; he has a marvelous way with words and with making a sentence "get up and walk away."

Fabian

Another servant of some importance in Lady Olivia's house.

Valentine and Curio

Two gentlemen who attend Duke Orsino.

A Sea Captain

He appears in only one scene. He helps Viola with her disguise.

SUMMARIES AND COMMENTARIES

ACT I – SCENE 1

Summary

Orsino, the Duke of Illyria, is sitting in his palace and enjoying himself by listening to music. He is in love and is in a whimsical, romantic mood, luxuriating in the various emotions which the music evokes. But he impulsively decides that he has heard enough, and after sending the musicians away, he expounds on the subject of love. Curio, one of his pages, asks his master if he wouldn't like to hunt; perhaps exercise will cure his master's soulful, philosophical moodiness. Orsino replies that he would like to hunt – but he would like to hunt the lovely Olivia, to whom he has sent another of his pages, Valentine, as an emissary. At that moment, Valentine enters. But he brings such bad news that he begs "not [to] be admitted": Olivia's brother has died, and she has vowed to mourn her brother's death for *seven years*. Surprisingly, the news does not dampen Orsino's spirit. He rhapsodizes on how a girl with such sensitivity can express her emotions; if she "hath a heart of that fine frame," he says, then she would be even more devoted and loyal to a lover.

Commentary

Twelfth Night has always been one of Shakespeare's most popular plays on the stage. On a first reading of the play, some students find the play difficult to come to grips with. This is because so much of the delight of the play comes from viewing the play. One must imagine the opening of the play with musicians entering and playing lovely music of a languid and melancholy nature to match the mood and personality of Duke Orsino's mood.

The general setting of the play is also significant. Shakespeare always set his comedies in faraway places so as to emphasize the ethereal quality of the romance. The name "Illyria" would be as little known to his audience as it is to today's average person; the fact that such a place did in fact exist on the Adriatic coast is of no importance to the play, for the name itself evokes images of faraway places filled with intrigues and love, and this is the concept that is emphasized throughout the play by the extensive use of music. In some productions, in addition to the songs played and sung on the stage, languid background music is played throughout the Comedy.

The Duke is in love, and his famous first lines announce this feeling:

> If music be the food of love, play on!
> Give me excess of it, that, surfeiting,
> The appetite may sicken, and so die.
>
> (1-3)

But the Duke is not in love with any one particular person (even though it would be foolish not to acknowledge, of course, the Lady Olivia); but most of all, the Duke is in love with love itself; after all, the Lady Olivia has rejected his protestations of love, and yet he continues to insist that she marry him. The Duke thoroughly delights in giving himself up to the exquisite delights of his own passions, but actually he does little to try to possess the object of his affections. In fact, this is the reason why he will later use Viola (Cesario) to do his courting for him.

The Duke's character is set in his first speech. At the same time that he indulges in the sentimental music, he impetuously grows tired of it and dismisses the musicians. The Duke then evokes the metaphor of the sea, which he likens to love. The sea is *vast*, as is the

Duke's capacity for love, but the sea is also changeable, unstable, and constantly shifting its mien. At the end of the Comedy, the Duke, significantly, will shift his love from the Lady Olivia to Viola within a moment; thus we should not be disturbed by this quick change. Feste later compares the Duke's love to an opal, a gem which constantly changes its color according to the nature of the light.

When we hear that the Lady Olivia is going to mourn her brother for seven years, her desire to remain "cloistered like a nun" for seven years identifies her as a person of extreme romantic sentimentality, one who is not in touch with the real world; thus, she is a romantic counterpart to Duke Orsino. When the Duke hears the news, he is pleased: if she can remain devoted to her *brother* for so long, it means that she has a constant heart; therefore, she will be constant to a lover forever, when the time comes. The Duke then lies down; he goes to his "sweet beds of flowers" (usually an ottoman or lounge) in order to sleep and dream, believing that "love thoughts lie rich when canopied with bowers." In this short opening scene, we have seen the Duke restless and enamored of love, tired of love, and finally ready to sleep and dream of love.

ACT I – SCENE 2

Summary

Viola and a sea captain and several sailors enter. They have been shipwrecked on the seacoast of Illyria and have barely escaped drowning. The captain congratulates Viola on not being drowned, for he tells her that when their ship split in half, he saw her brother, Sebastian, tie himself to a mast; yet even that, he fears, did not save Sebastian, for he saw him and the mast borne away on the waves. According to the captain, there is a slim chance that Sebastian survived, but there is a strong possibility that only the captain, Viola, and these few sailors are the sole survivors. Viola is appreciative of the captain's kind, if cautious, optimism; she gives him some gold coins and asks him if he has any idea where they are. The captain does; he knows Illyria well. He was born and reared here, and he tells Viola that the country is governed by a "noble Duke," Duke Orsino. Viola recognizes the name; her father spoke of him. The Duke is a bachelor, she believes.

The captain is not so sure that this fact is still true; he says that according to current gossip, the Duke has been seeking the love of "fair Olivia," but he says that Olivia is a virgin and that she is determined to remain so. Following the death of Olivia's father (a year ago) and the death of her brother (just recently), Olivia forswore men altogether.

The story intrigues Viola; she herself is now in mourning for her brother, Sebastian, and nothing would please her more than to serve Olivia. The captain, however, says that such a plan is impossible. Olivia will see no one. For a moment, Viola ponders, then she devises an ingenious scheme. She will disguise herself as a young eunuch, and she will pay the captain handsomely for his aid if he presents her to Duke Orsino. She will sing for the Duke, play any number of musical instruments for him and — in short — she will ingratiate herself in his household. The captain agrees, and they exit.

Commentary

With the shift of this scene to the seacoast of Illyria, we meet another principal character in the Comedy — Viola — and in meeting her, we hear more about the Lady Olivia, and even though their names are almost perfect anagrams (a rearrangement of the same letters in the names), and even though they are in similar dramatic situations in this play, they are vastly different women. Both of them have recently been orphaned, and, to all outward semblances, both have lost a brother and are therefore alone in the world. But here the similarity ends. Olivia is indulging in her grief, but whereas Viola deeply grieves for her brother, she is still able to function in the practical world. Unlike Olivia, Viola, shipwrecked and alone, does not have time to indulge in her grief. Being a shipwrecked virgin maid on a strange shore and knowing no one, she must use her wit, her intelligence, and her ability to analyze situations and characters. Consequently, Viola decides to disguise herself as a man for a very practical purpose — to assure her own protection in an alien world which would not respect a young virgin maiden. And with the assumption of this disguise, we will have the beginning of a complicated series of disguises which will run throughout the remainder of the Comedy.

Viola's uncanny ability to intuit other people's ideas enables her to trust the sea captain; he can help her carry out her plans and keep her identity secret. Without his trust, her plans would fail, and after she has assumed her disguise, she uses it to its fullest potential – that is, she never passes up the opportunity to use her disguise in order to make puns and double entendres for parodies and satires and, ultimately, to comment subtly on the disguised biological difference between herself and the Lady Olivia. In other words, while the disguise provides Viola with security and protection, it also allows her to utilize her wit for her own enjoyment and also for the enjoyment of the audience.

ACT I – SCENE 3

Summary

At Olivia's house, Sir Toby Belch, Olivia's uncle, is criticizing his niece for mourning the death of her brother so profusely. He says to her serving girl, Maria, that his niece is melodramatically over-reacting, and he thoroughly disapproves. Maria disapproves of several things herself: she disapproves of Sir Toby's arriving at such a late hour, dressing so slovenly, and drinking so much. Only yesterday, Olivia complained of these things, plus the fact that Sir Toby brought someone who he thinks is *the* perfect suitor to the house, Sir Andrew Aguecheek. Despite Maria's calling Aguecheek a "fool and a prodigal," Sir Toby is proud of the chap – a fitting suitor for his niece: Aguecheek, he says, receives three thousand ducats a year, plays the violincello, and speaks several languages. Maria is not impressed. To her, the man is reputed to be a gambler, a quarreler, a coward, and a habitual drunkard.

When Sir Andrew joins them, there follows a brief exchange of jests, most of them at Sir Andrew's expense. Maria leaves, and the two men discuss Sir Andrew's chances as a prospective suitor of Olivia. Sir Andrew is discouraged and ready to ride home tomorrow, but Sir Toby persuades him to prolong his visit for another month, especially since Sir Andrew delights in masques and revels and, as Sir Toby points out, Sir Andrew is a superb dancer and an acrobat, as well. Laughing and joking, the two men leave the stage. It is obvious that Sir Toby has a secret and mysterious purpose for wanting to persuade Sir Andrew to stay and woo the fair Olivia.

Commentary

With this scene, we are introduced to still another set of characters: in the modern idiom, we have already met the "upstairs" characters; now we meet the "downstairs" characters. Sir Toby Belch, Sir Andrew Aguecheek, and Maria form the subplot that counterbalances the main plot. Sir Toby Belch, as his name implies, is characterized by his heavy drinking and by his obese, corpulent frame. In an earlier play, Shakespeare created a similar type of character in Sir John Falstaff (See *Henry IV, Part I* and *Part II*); this character was extremely popular with Elizabethan audiences, and Sir Toby is reminiscent of the earlier Sir John; both are plump, jolly knights with a penchant for drinking, merrymaking, and foolery of all types. In this play, Sir Toby spends most of his time complimenting Sir Andrew so that the latter will continue to supply him with money for drinking and cavorting. Sir Toby's niece, we discover, is too withdrawn in her melodramatic mourning to be aware of the partying going on in her house, but when she does become aware of it, she disapproves and relies upon her steward, Malvolio, to keep her household in order; thus, Malvolio will soon become the butt of the partymakers' jokes.

Maria, another member of the subplot, is Olivia's vivacious, clever, and mischievous maid. She comes from a Shakespearean tradition of servants who are wittier and cleverer than the people who surround them. Thus, she will be seen to be far more witty than Sir Andrew Aguecheek is, and he will become the object of her many jokes and puns, but he will never realize the extent to which Maria ridicules him.

Sir Andrew Aguecheek is necessary for the plot mainly because he is in possession of three thousand ducats a year, and Sir Toby is anxious to remain on good terms with him so as to be a recipient of the eccentric knight's beneficence. Consequently, he continually plots ways to make the knight think that Olivia is indeed receptive to the romantic overtures of the tall, skinny, ridiculous knight. Now we know that two vastly different people, Duke Orsino and Sir Andrew Aguecheek, are both seeking the hand of the Lady Olivia. Later, Malvolio will become a third "suitor," by a ruse played upon him by Maria and her cohorts.

ACT I – SCENE 4

Summary

In Duke Orsino's palace, one of his pages, Valentine, enters, accompanied by Viola, disguised as a young eunuch, Cesario. By their conversation, we realize that after only three days, Cesario has already become a great favorite with the Duke. In fact, Viola has won Orsino's confidence and favor so thoroughly that when "Cesario" enters, Orsino sends the others away so that he and Cesario might be alone. He asks Cesario to do him a very special, very personal favor. Cesario is to be the Duke's messenger, his proxy, and carry notes of love from Orsino to Olivia. Cesario is to explain in detail the passion which Orsino has for Olivia and, in addition, Cesario is to enact Orsino's "woes." Furthermore, because Cesario himself is so beautifully handsome, Orsino believes that his avowals of love will be all the better received. His reasoning is that his love messages will entice the fair Olivia favorably because they will be presented in such a handsome package, as it were. Orsino also says that if Cesario is successful, he will be well rewarded; he will "live as freely as thy lord/ To call his fortune thine."

Cesario is reluctant; in an aside, he reveals that "he" (Viola in disguise) has fallen in love with Orsino. Ironically, as Cesario, Viola will be doing some wooing for a man whom she would gladly have as a husband herself.

Commentary

This scene shows us that Viola has been completely successful in carrying out her plan to become a member of Duke Orsino's household. Within a period of only three days she has completely captivated the Duke, who has taken a fancy to her and is now not only employing her as his personal messenger, but he has also confided his innermost thoughts to her – that is, he has confided them to "Cesario."

At the opening of the scene, Valentine informs Cesario that he is likely to be advanced in the Duke's service. This prompts Cesario to ask if the Duke is sometimes "inconstant" in his favors. Viola is hoping that the Duke will ultimately be constant to her – and yet she is also hoping that the Duke will be inconstant in his affections for Olivia; it is not, however, until the last line of this scene that we discover that in these three days Viola has fallen in love with the Duke. Part of the comic situation here involves the dramatic irony that Viola (in disguise) is forced to try to win Olivia for Duke Orsino when in reality, she would like to shed her disguise and be his wife herself.

At the end of the scene, Viola cries out, "Whoe'er I woo, myself would be his wife." This statement aligns Viola then with the other romantic lovers. She differs from them only by the fact that she is in constant touch with reality and can therefore evaluate her position.

ACT I – SCENE 5

Summary

In Olivia's house, Maria and Feste, the jester, are exchanging quips. Olivia, she tells him, is piqued because of Feste's absence. She jokingly tells him that Olivia may hang him, but Feste is not intimidated. "Many a good hanging prevents a bad marriage," he retorts. He delights in teasing Maria, whom he is complimenting in mock extravagance when Olivia and her steward, Malvolio, enter.

The two of them are very grave and very serious. Olivia orders Feste away, but Feste stays on, determined to amuse his mistress; he launches into a series of jokes that eventually amuse Olivia, despite her serious mien. But Feste's merriment does *not* amuse the pompous and humorless Malvolio. Malvolio says that the jester is a weak and sick man, as is his wit. Malvolio's arrogant scorn delights Feste, and he easily parries Malvolio's weak wit and, thereby, impresses Olivia. She tells Malvolio that he is "sick of self-love" and "distempered." Jesters, she says, do not slander; it is their craft, a harmless craft, and that Feste is only reproving Malvolio.

Maria enters and tells them that a fair young man from Duke Orsino has arrived and wishes an interview with Olivia, but that he is being detained by Olivia's uncle, Sir Toby. Olivia's temper flares. She will *not* be wooed by the Duke – nor by anyone else. She doesn't care what the messenger is told; any excuse will do. She wants to see *no* suitors, she says, and she tells Maria to send the young man away immediately. While Maria and Malvolio are gone, Sir Toby appears. He is drunk, and Feste has a marvellous opportunity to ape Olivia's old uncle's drunken antics. Olivia is amused by Feste's cleverness, and her mood softens; she sends Feste to look after her uncle after he exits. She wants to make sure that nothing serious happens to him in his inebriated condition.

Malvolio enters and tells Olivia that the "fair young man" is indeed "fair" and "young," and that he is, in addition, persistent. Olivia relents and agrees to see the lad—as long as Maria is present. She then veils her face before he enters.

Viola, disguised as Cesario, enters and begins his mission by addressing Olivia with many compliments, while adroitly avoiding answering Olivia's questions about his status and background, for Olivia is very inquisitive about this fair, young "man." Cesario continues, and Olivia at last feels so comfortable with the fellow that she dismisses Maria, and the two of them begin to speak of Duke Orsino and his status as a suitor for Olivia's hand in marriage. Olivia is eventually persuaded to unveil herself, and she presents her beautiful face to Cesario—to which "he" responds playfully and most positively: "Excellently done, if God did all." Cesario then laments that the owner of such beauty is indeed cruel if she would carry her "graces to the grave" and "leave the world no copy." He reassures her of Orsino's love, but Olivia says that she doubts that Orsino's love is of any real depth. He does not truly know her; therefore, he must press his suit no further. Yet, on the other hand, if *Cesario* wishes to come again, Olivia will be most happy to see him. She hands the young man a purse of money for his troubles, but Cesario refuses it. Indignantly, he says that he is no "fee'd post." He bids Olivia farewell—farewell to her "fair cruelty."

Absolutely intrigued with young Cesario, Olivia calls to Malvolio. She tells him to follow Orsino's messenger and to return a ring that he left behind. She also tells Malvolio to inform Cesario that if the youth returns tomorrow, she will explain in detail why Orsino's suit is impossible.

Olivia has fallen in love. The ring is a ruse; Cesario left no ring. Olivia is merely trying to arrange a rendezvous tomorrow between herself and the handsome young envoy from Duke Orsino.

Commentary

Most elegant houses of this time would include, in addition to a large number of servants of different standings, a person who was considered the official "fool," "jester," or "clown." Many critics make a distinction between these terms but even Shakespeare uses them indiscriminately. Traditionally, in Renaissance terms, the word *clown* often referred mainly to rustics such as those found in *A Midsummer-Night's Dream*, and a person such as Feste would more appropriately be termed a "fool" (a court jester). Here, Feste opens the scene with the witty servant Maria, and they are engaged in a verbal sparring match. The two are very well matched; Maria is a mischievous, quick-witted person, and Feste has a mind like quicksilver. The pattern of their verbal humor and interchanges is executed in a rapid give-and-take repartee, which is extremely effective on stage.

The entrance of the Countess Olivia has been long awaited. We have heard about her since the opening scene of the act, and now finally at the end of Act I, she makes her first appearance. We are not disappointed. She is beautiful and poised, and she possesses a commanding presence as she immediately reprimands the clown for his lack of seriousness at a time when she is in mourning. As the scene progresses, we see that Olivia shows great intelligence; she is very adept in verbal skills, she appreciates the magnificent humor of the clown, especially when it is aimed at the dour and grave Malvolio, and she is also very practical in disapproving of her uncle's drunkenness and loud belching. And while she acknowledges that the Duke is handsome, wealthy, devoted, learned, and refined—in other words, everything a lady could desire—yet she feels that she cannot love him. Later in the scene, we learn that one of her reasons could be that the Duke exhibits extreme melodramatics in his message to Olivia. When Cesario delivers the Duke's message that he loves Olivia "with adorations, with fertile tears,/ With groans that thunder love, with sighs of fire," this declaration represents gross sentimentality; the phrasing is a perfect description of the rhetorical and superficial nature of Duke Orsino's love.

At her entrance, Olivia immediately instructs someone to "take the fool [Feste] away." She finds him to be a "dry fool"—that is, Olivia is in mourning, and foolery ill becomes her at this time. When the fool asks for permission to prove his lady a fool, she grants him permission to do so, and eventually Olivia appreciates the fool's wit and logic; in fact, she is sharp with Malvolio, who disparages the fool and wonders how his mistress can take delight in such a rascal. Again, Malvolio shows that he has no sense of humor; he constantly tries to keep the entire household in an atmosphere of gravity and oppression. This prepares the audience to take great delight in the trick that will be played on him later.

When Cesario arrives at the gate, notice that Olivia will have nothing to do with this messenger. Yet Olivia changes her mind about seeing the messenger when she hears the description of the youth given her by Malvolio, a description which whets her imagination; suddenly she desires very much to see him, but she is not anxious to reveal this in front of the dour Malvolio. Thus, we realize that Olivia's guise of mourning for her brother is only another of the many disguises that are employed during this Comedy – that is, Lady Olivia used the excuse of her brother's death as a pretext for singling herself out and making herself interesting, and certainly news of her excessive mourning has been carried throughout the country, as we saw in all the preceding scenes.

When Cesario is admitted, further masks and disguises are used to their fullest. First, Olivia has a veil over her face which disguises her true appearance. Viola herself, of course, is in disguise as the young Cesario and, furthermore, as Cesario, she is playing a part because as Cesario, she has memorized a speech that is to be delivered to Olivia. Then, too, there is an abundance of play on words, constantly emphasizing how Olivia is usurping her own role and that Cesario wants only to present the *heart* of the message, which is to play on Olivia's *heart*, and when Cesario finally finishes his speech, he says that he holds an olive, the sign of peace in his hand. Note that "olive" is a derivation of Olivia's name and ultimately, by the end of this scene, Cesario will figuratively hold Olivia in "his" hands, since she will by then be enamored of the youth. Cesario must, of necessity, be a good wooer or else lose favor with Duke Orsino. Therefore, there is such a passionate intensity in his pleading that Olivia is struck not so much by the message (which is trite, old and hackneyed), but by the messenger (who is young, passionate, and good-looking). At the same time, Cesario senses that Olivia is too proud to be wooed by proxy, but he attempts to do so anyway. After the message is delivered, Olivia is oblivious to it, but she is so entranced by the messenger that she offers a purse filled with money. Cesario refuses the gift indignantly; he is no fee-accepting person: "*I* am no fee'd post, Lady; keep your purse. My master, not myself, lacks recompense."

After Cesario has left, Olivia remembers Cesario's proud declaration: "I am a gentleman." Olivia, in fact, savors remembering
Cesario's entire conversation; she is aware that she is falling in love
with the "boy," and she wonders if it is possible that Orsino is pre-
tending to be Cesario. Her desire to find out and her desire to see the
young "boy" again causes her to perpetrate a ruse to bring the youth
back to her. We know that this is a trick; Cesario left no ring behind,
but this is the safest way that Olivia can try to persuade the youth to
return.

At the end of Act I, Olivia is in a delicious state of incipient love
after having rejected the Duke's offer of love. She accepts her fate,
whatever it may be, and exits, thinking of young Cesario in the
warmest terms. The situation is now extremely complicated: Olivia
loves a girl (Viola) masquerading as a boy (Cesario), while Duke Orsino loves Olivia, who rejects him, and he is in turn loved by a girl
(Viola) who, to the Duke, is merely a young man whose company he
delights in.

ACT II – SCENE 1

Summary

The second act begins on the seacoast of Illyria. Viola's twin
brother, Sebastian, was not drowned after all. He survived the shipwreck and enters on stage talking with Antonio, a sea captain (not
the same sea captain who managed to reach shore with Viola). Sebastian, like his sister Viola, is deeply grieved; he is sure that Viola was
lost at sea and perished in the storm. He blames the stars and "the
malignancy of [his] fate" for his dark mood and his misfortune. He
turns to the sea captain, and, feeling that he can be straightforward
with him because of what they have both just experienced, he tells
the captain that he wants to be alone. He needs solitude because of
his terrible grief; his troubles are many, and he fears that they will
spread like an illness and "distemper" the sea captain's mood. He
cares too much for the captain to unburden his woes on him.

Antonio, however, will not leave Sebastian; his friendship for
the young man is strong enough to withstand Sebastian's emotionalism. Sebastian's composure suddenly breaks, and he bewails his
lot; if Antonio had not saved him, he would now be dead at the bot-
tom of the sea, alongside his beloved sister. "If the heavens had been

pleased," his fate would have been the same as his sister's. He then recalls his sister's beauty, and he remembers her keen mind, a mind that was extraordinary and enviable. At this point, Antonio protests. Sebastian was correct when he spoke earlier of his dark moodiness being able to "distemper" Antonio's temperament. The sea captain says that Sebastian's lamentations are "bad entertainment," a fact that Sebastian quickly realizes and quickly apologizes for.

Antonio changes the subject to matters more practical and more immediate. He asks Sebastian if he can be the young man's servant. That single favor would please him immensely. That single favor, however, Sebastian cannot grant him, for as much as he would like to do so, he dare not take Antonio with him. His destination is Duke Orsino's court and Antonio has "many enemies" in Orsino's court. Yet "come what may," Antonio says that he will always treasure his friendship with Sebastian. Thus, he *will* go with Sebastian. Antonio's devotion to Sebastian is admirable; he recognizes the dangers ahead if he follows Sebastian to Orsino's palace, but after the horrors of the shipwreck, future "danger shall seem sport."

Commentary

This scene takes us away from the regal households and out to the seashore on another part of the coast of Illyria. The two new characters who are introduced, Sebastian and Antonio, form the third plot line of the Comedy. Sebastian is Viola's twin brother whom she believes was probably drowned at sea, and this fact will create comic complications, which will be resolved in the fifth act. Like his sister, Sebastian is kind and good-looking. When Sebastian describes his sister as a lady "though it was said she much resembled me, was yet of many accounted beautiful," we are being prepared for the confusion later in the play when Sebastian will be mistaken for Cesario (Viola), and Viola (as Cesario) will be mistaken for Sebastian by Antonio, the sea captain.

Sebastian will appear throughout the rest of the Comedy as more impulsive and more emotional than his twin sister; for example, he will consent to marry a woman (Olivia) whom he has just met – an act of extreme impetuosity. But yet we must assume that Sebastian possesses many manly and good qualities to have attracted the loyalty of such a stalwart man as the sea captain, who decides to risk his life to accompany the handsome young lad to Duke Orsino's court.

ACT II – SCENE 2

Summary

Viola, still in disguise as Cesario, comes on stage and is followed by Malvolio, who catches up with the lad and asks him if he is indeed the young man who was with the Countess Olivia only a short time ago. Cesario admits that it was he, and Malvolio holds out a ring to him – seemingly a ring that Duke Orsino sent to Olivia, one which Cesario left behind by mistake. Malvolio adds sarcastically that Cesario would have saved Malvolio the time and trouble of returning it if Cesario had not been so absent-minded. Scornfully, Malvolio tells Cesario to return to his master, Orsino, and tell him that Olivia "will none of him," and furthermore he warns Cesario that he should "never be so hardy to come again in his [Orsino's] affairs."

Cesario is dumbfounded by Malvolio's high-handed manner; then, matching Malvolio's insolence, he says, "I'll none of it." Malvolio is incensed at Cesario's haughty manner and flings the ring to the ground; if Cesario wants it and "if it be worth stooping for, there it lies." With that, he exits abruptly.

Left alone, Viola ponders all that has happened; she is absolutely certain that she left no ring with Olivia, yet why does Olivia believe that she did and, moreover, why did she send Malvolio with such urgency to return it? Then she realizes what may have happened, and she is horrified: can it be possible that Olivia has fallen in love with Viola's boyish disguise? She is aghast: "fortune forbid my outside have not charmed her!" Thinking back on their interview, however, she clearly recalls that Olivia certainly "made good view of me; indeed, so much/ That sure methought her eyes had lost her tongue."

The evidence is clear. Olivia has indeed fallen in love with Cesario; when she spoke to the young man, she spoke in starts and spurts, and her manner was vague and distracted. Now "the winning of her passion" has sent Malvolio after the "boy" whom she believes to be the object of her love.

Viola pities Olivia; it would be better for the poor Olivia to "love a dream." Viola recognizes that "disguise . . . art a wickedness." She aptly calls disguise a "pregnant enemy," an enemy able to play havoc with "women's waxen hearts." Like Olivia, Viola too is a woman. She knows the anguish of love: "Our frailty is the cause, not we," she meditates, "for such are we made of."

This is a dreadfully complicated knot. Viola loves her master, Orsino, who loves the beautiful but disdainful Olivia, who loves the handsome Cesario (who is not a man at all, but is Viola, in disguise). Viola calls on Time to untangle this knot, for she is incapable of doing so herself; "it is too hard a knot for me to untie."

Commentary

At the end of Act I, Olivia sent Malvolio to catch up with Cesario and return a ring that Cesario did *not* leave behind. In this short scene, Malvolio is seen returning the ring in a very scornful, haughty, and arrogant manner. The scene serves in part to bring out Malvolio's rudeness and his ill nature. He is extremely insolent to a youth who has caused him no personal injury. His unwarranted enmity is seen in the manner in which he delivers the ring. Malvolio's action here again prepares the reader for delight in the tricks that will later be played on this insolent man who shows nothing but scorn for any person who is not above him in social status.

While this scene does not advance the plot, it does show us how intricately Viola is caught up in the entanglement. She suddenly realizes that Olivia has fallen in love with an exterior facade – and not with the inner person. This realization allows her to comment on the "frailty" of women who are constantly deceived by disguises of one sort or another. When Viola cries out: "Disguise, I see thou art a wickedness,/ Wherein the pregnant enemy does much," she speaks with allusions about the "wickedness" that arises from a woman's being constantly deceived by disguises, ever since Eve was first deceived in the Garden of Eden. Yet, Viola must retain her disguise because, as a girl alone in a foreign country, she would be powerless to defend herself, as we see later when the cowardly Sir Aguecheek threatens her.

ACT II – SCENE 3

Summary

At Olivia's house, it is late and Sir Toby and Sir Andrew have been drinking, or "revelling," as they call it. They are noisily celebrating – reciting fragments of songs, Latin sayings, and old country proverbs. They play at logic: Sir Andrew says in all inebriated seriousness that "to be up late is to be up late." Sir Toby absolutely *dis*agrees: "a false conclusion," he pronounces, and a flaw in reasoning, a vexation which he dislikes as much as he does an empty beer mug. Then he launches into an involved, implausible, and ridiculous diatribe involving the hours of the day and of the night and the four elements, and ends by praising Sir Andrew for being such a superb scholar because Sir Andrew agrees with Sir Toby's final conclusion—that "life . . . consists of eating and drinking," which reminds Sir Toby that what they both need is another drink. Thus he bellows loudly for "Marian" (Maria) to fetch them "a stoup of wine."

Feste, the jester, has not gone to bed and is delighted to come in and discover a party going on. They all joke uproariously in broad comedy about their all being asses, and then they attempt to approximate the acerbic flair of high comedy, but their bits and pieces of joking become so disjointed that it is impossible to know exactly what they are laughing about, nor is it terribly important. The point is, they are having manly, goodhearted drunken fun and, therefore, they indulge quite naturally in some loud singing. Very naturally, one of the first songs is a love song. It is sung by Feste and begins "O mistress mine" and concerns men wooing their true loves. The second verse praises the experience of love: love is an act, to be acted *upon*; "tis not hereafter." The future, according to the song, is unsure; therefore, lovers should kiss for "youth's a stuff [which] will not endure." The philosophy of the song is agreeable to all, as is Feste's "mellifluous voice," according to the tipsy Sir Andrew. Sir Toby criticizes Feste's breath, pondering momentarily on the possibility of one's being able to hear with one's nose. Then in the next breath, he suggests that they celebrate so thoroughly that they will "rouse the night-owl" and make the sky itself (the "welkin") dance. Sir Andrew thinks that this is a splendid idea: "I am dog at a catch," he cries out, meaning that he is clever at singing. Yet no sooner do they begin, than their tongues tumble over the words "knaves" and "knights," two completely different kinds of men, and they attempt to begin all over again when Maria comes in. She warns them that their "caterwauling," their wailing like three sex-starved tomcats, is going to get them thrown out of the place. If Olivia is awakened, she will have her steward, Malvolio, toss them all out. Neither Sir Toby nor Sir Andrew pays any attention whatsoever to her; they are too far gone in their cups, and they call Olivia a "Cataian," (a bitch) and call Malvolio a "Peg-a-Ramsey." This latter slur is very insulting, referring to an over-the-hill, henpecked impotent man who woefully longs for the long-gone days when men sported yellow hose and wooed the village maids. Sir Toby begins a new song, with the words "On the twelfth day of December . . ." and suddenly they are all startled to see a figure in the doorway. It is Malvolio.

He is haughty and as imperious as Maria warned them that he would be. He tells them that Olivia has said that either they must quiet down or else they must leave the house. Sir Toby and Feste mock Malvolio's edicts with satiric farewells, and Malvolio becomes furious. He is scandalized to hear such insults in his lady Olivia's house. He turns on Maria and attempts to shame her for allowing such misbehavior. He shall report *her* part in all this "uncivil rule." He warns them that they should make no mistake about what he plans to do. Their insubordination will be reported – immediately!

Resentful of Malvolio's lordly posings, the drunken merry-makers loudly applaud Maria's proposed plan to outwit the sharp-tongued, all-important Malvolio. She will forge a letter in Olivia's handwriting ("some obscure epistles of love") that will contain soulful, sighing admirations for "the color of [Malvolio's] beard, the shape of his leg, the manner of his gait, the expression of his eye, forehead, and complexion" – in short, in a very brief time, Malvolio will mistakenly believe that Olivia is in love with him. "A sport royal," Maria predicts. With that, she tells them to hide and eavesdrop on Malvolio when "he shall find the letter." She then bids them goodnight; the three men are intoxicated at the thought of what will ensue. Malvolio will be made a fool of; he has needed such an experience for a long time, and this exciting prospect, of course, calls for a drink.

Commentary

Much of the spontaneity of this scene is lost to the reader of the Comedy; however, on the stage, this is a hilarious comic masterpiece. It is a jovial company; first, Sir Toby and Sir Andrew are carousing in drunken, noisy celebration and are soon joined by Feste, who will also provide some songs. Then Maria, complaining at first, finally joins the celebration. The mood is one of partying and indulgence as Maria keeps a constant lookout, for she knows that Malvolio would delight to report just such shenanigans to the Lady Olivia. The rapid, witty exchanges are difficult for the modern audience, but what emerges of major importance is that Sir Toby is not just an average drunk; he is indeed a true wit, whose lines addressed to Sir Andrew establish the fact that the latter is a gull and an ignoramus.

The entrance of Malvolio is particularly comic. Remember that Malvolio is tall, skinny, and bald. Traditionally, he appears dressed in his nightgown and night cap, and he stands above the party makers as a magnificently ridiculous figure carrying a lit candle in a candlestick. It is difficult to take his authority seriously since he looks so ridiculous. Sir Toby and Feste dance around this foolish figure, and finally, when Malvolio reminds Sir Toby that he can be thrown out of the household, Malvolio has taken a step too far. It should be remembered that in the Elizabethan stratified society, Malvolio, while he is a steward, is inferior to Sir Toby in *social* rank, and whatever limitations Sir Toby may have, he *is* a knight and he *is* Lady Olivia's uncle. Thus after Malvolio's threat, Sir Toby asks him, "Art any more than a steward?" Then the essential conflict between the two is stated by Sir Toby: "Dost thou think, because thou art virtuous, there shall be no more cakes and ale?" This final statement characterizes perfectly the two types of people in the world: There are the Malvolios who would have everyone be as austere and priggish as he is, and then there are the Sir Tobys who will always find pleasure in life. The term "cakes and ale" has become famous as a phrase describing pleasure-loving people. After Sir Toby puts Malvolio in his place, Malvolio turns to Maria to reprimand her, and then he exits.

The remainder of the scene deals with the plot which they will all concoct in order to get even with Malvolio, using the knowledge that Malvolio is such an egotist that he would readily believe that a love letter, ostensibly sent from Olivia, was addressed to him. Thus, as the scene ends, we are prepared not only for the complicated love triangle, but also for the duping of the haughty Malvolio. We also see that Sir Toby is aware of an affection that Maria has for him, and at the end of the Comedy, we will learn that these two are married.

ACT II – SCENE 4

Summary

At Orsino's palace, the Duke is gathered together with Cesario (Viola), Curio, and others, and he says that he would like to hear a song, a certain "old and antique" song that he heard last night; the song seemed to "relieve [his] passion much." Feste, the jester, is not there to sing it, however, so Orsino sends Curio out to find him and, while Curio is gone, Orsino calls Cesario to him. He tells the young lad that "if ever [Cesario] shalt love," then he should remember how Orsino suffered while he experienced love's sweet pangs. Orsino tells Cesario that Orsino himself is the sad epitome of all lovers—"unstaid and skittish"—except when he recalls "the constant image" of his beloved. Cesario hints that love has already enthroned itself within him, and Orsino remarks that he believes that Cesario is indeed correct. He can tell by looking at the boy that his "eye/ Hath stay'd upon some favour that it loves." Cesario acknowledges that this is true. The Duke is intrigued; he is curious about the woman who has caught Cesario's fancy, and he begins to question the lad.

Cesario says that the object of his love is a great deal like Orsino, a confession that makes Orsino scoff: "She is not worth thee, then," he says. When he learns that Cesario's "beloved" is about Orsino's own age, he becomes indignant. A woman, he says, should take someone "elder than herself." He says that women, by nature, are not able to love with the same intensity as a young man is able to love; women need to find themselves a steady, doggedly devoted older man whose passions are burned low and, thus, more equal to hers. Cesario, Orsino suggests, needs to find a very young virgin, one who has just blossomed, "for women are as a rose [and] being once displayed, do fall that very hour." Cesario sadly agrees; women, he says, often "die, even when they to perfection grow."

Curio and Feste enter then, and Feste is more than happy to sing the song that he sang last night. He urges Cesario, in particular, to take note of it for although it is "old and plain," it is a song that is well known. Spinsters sing it, as do young maidens; its theme concerns the simple truth of love's innocence. The song begins, "Come away, come away, death . . ." (which is certainly a melancholy evocation) and goes on to lament unrequited love—of which Orsino and Viola (and Olivia) all suffer. The lover of the song is a young man who has been "slain" by "a fair cruel maid," and, his heart broken, he asks for a shroud of white to encase his body. He wants no flowers strewn on his black coffin; nor does he want friends nor mourners present when he is lowered into the grave. In fact, he wants to be buried in a secret place so that no other "sad true lover" will chance to find his grave and find reason to weep there. The emphasis here is on the *innocence of love*, and our focus is on poor Viola, who has innocently fallen in love with Duke Orsino, who believes that she is only a handsome young man, to whom he feels "fatherly."

Orsino gives Feste some money for singing the mournful ballad, and, in return, Feste praises his good and generous master and then exits. The Duke then excuses the others, and when he and Cesario are alone, he turns to the boy and tells him that he must return to Olivia and her "sovereign cruelty." He tells Cesario that he *must* convince Olivia that Orsino's love is "more noble than the world." It is not her riches which he seeks (her "quantity of dirty lands"); instead, he prizes her as a "queen of gems." It is his *soul* which loves her. When Cesario asks what he should say if Olivia protests that she absolutely cannot love Orsino, the Duke refuses to accept such an answer.

Cesario then grows bold and tells Orsino that perhaps there is "some lady" who has "as great a pang of heart" for him as he has for Olivia. Orsino refuses to acknowledge that *women* can love with the passion that *men* can:

> . . . no woman's sides
> Can bide the beating of so strong a passion
> As love doth give my heart; no woman's heart
> So big, to hold so much.
>
> (92-95)

True love, he says, using a typically Elizabethan analogy, lies in one's liver, and a woman's love lies only on the tip of her tongue. Women may talk sweetly, but women cannot "suffer surfeit, cloyment and revolt," pains of the liver which are reserved for only men. He wants to make it perfectly clear to Cesario that there is "no compare/ Between that love a woman can bear me/ And that I owe Olivia."

Cesario now becomes bolder still and says that women can indeed love with as much passion as men can. He knows it to be so, for his father had a daughter who loved a man with as much passion as Cesario himself could love Orsino—that is, *if* Cesario were a woman. Then Cesario realizes that perhaps he has said enough on the subject, but when Orsino inquires further concerning the history of this "sister," Cesario's imagination is rekindled. He returns to the theme of the unrequited lover and conjures up a sad tale about his "sister" who loved so purely and so passionately and so privately that love became "like a worm in the bud" of her youth and fed "on her damask cheek." Turning to Orsino, he says, "We men may say more, swear more," but talk is often empty. His sister died, Cesario sighs, and now he is "all the daughters of my father's house,/ And all the brothers too." With this cryptic statement in mind, the Duke gives Cesario a jewel. He is to present it to Olivia, and he is to "bide no denay" – that is, he is not to take *No* for an answer. Orsino is determined to have Olivia's love.

Commentary

In contrast to all of the shenanigans involved in the subplot of the last scene, this scene shifts abruptly back to Duke Orsino's palace, and, once again, the mood and atmosphere are re-established as the Duke again calls for music. We return to that same languid and indolent Duke; now, he asks for the old and antique song that he heard last night. Later in the scene, Feste will appear and sing the song "Come away, Come away, death." The theme of this lyric is the sadness unto death of a young man whose love for a fair, cruel maid is unrequited. (The Duke obviously sees a parallel between his and Lady Olivia's relationship in the song). The youth in the song dies of his love, and he hopes that no other sad, true lover shall find his grave for a similar reason – that is, because of unrequited love. The song is quaint and filled with conceits. Its melancholy artifice probably appeals to the Duke in his present mood, and it certainly suits the musical atmosphere of the play as a whole. Ironically, while the theme of the song expresses Duke Orsino's mood, it also expresses the mood of Olivia (who is unrequited in her love for Cesario), as well as that of Viola (who is unrequited in her love for Count Orsino).

At the end of the scene, when Cesario says, "My father had a daughter loved a man," this statement comes as close as Viola dares in expressing her love for Duke Orsino. The contrast is between her tormented, inner anguish and reasoned love and the Duke's exaggerated statements of love. While Viola's passion is less pretentious than the Duke's, it is nevertheless as deep and sincere.

The ending of the scene furthers the plot since Orsino once more *commands* Cesario to deliver a love message and a jewel to Olivia, thus setting up another encounter between the unrequited Olivia and the inaccessible Cesario (Viola).

ACT II – SCENE 5

Summary

Sir Toby, Sir Andrew, and Fabian (another of Olivia's servants) have agreed to meet in Olivia's garden, and as the scene begins, the three men enter, Sir Toby urging Fabian on. But Fabian, as we quickly realize, needs no urging; he is more than anxious to relish every minute of their plan to make a fool of Malvolio. Like Sir Toby and Sir Andrew, Fabian has his own quarrel with the prudish, sharp-tongued Malvolio. It seems that Malvolio reported to Olivia that Fabian was "bear-baiting," a popular (if cruel) Elizabethan sport and one which Fabian enjoys. Sir Toby predicts that very soon Malvolio will be the "bear," for the bait will soon be set. They do not have long to wait, for, as Sir Toby points out, "Here comes the little villain."

Before Malvolio comes onstage, however, Maria rushes in and makes sure that they are all well concealed in a "box-tree" (a long hedge trimmed to look like a box). Satisfied, she puts the forged love letter in the garden path, where Malvolio will be sure to find it. "The trout" (Malvolio), she vows, will be caught with "tickling" (having his vanity tickled).

When Malvolio enters, he is greedily weighing the possibility that Olivia may be falling in love with him. Maria herself, he says, confirmed such a notion, and he himself has heard Olivia say that if ever she should choose a husband, that man would be someone very much like Malvolio; also, Malvolio believes that Olivia treats him with more respect than she does any of her other suitors. The thought of Malvolio's being "*Count* Malvolio" overwhelms him. He conjures up visions of himself – married to Olivia for three months and lovingly letting her sleep in the morning while he, robed in a "velvet gown," rises from the bed and calls his officers to him. He imagines himself reminding his officers to remember their place. Then he would call for his "Cousin Toby," and while he is waiting, he would "frown the while," and toy with his watch or with "some rich jewel." He envisions Sir Toby approaching, curtsying and quaking, as Malvolio reminds him that because "fortune" has given Malvolio "this prerogative of speech," he will austerely command his "kinsman" to "amend [his] drunkenness." He will also inform Sir Toby that he "wastes the treasure of . . . time with a foolish knight" – a contemptuous slur at Sir Andrew.

At this point, Malvolio spies the "love note.' He reads it and is absolutely convinced that it was written by Olivia. The script and the phraseology are Olivia's, and the note also has her stamp that she uses for sealing letters. As he reads the poem of love, Malvolio ponders over its mystery. Olivia confesses that only "Jove knows" whom she truly loves; her lips cannot say and "no man must know." The first stanza is unclear, but Malvolio finds hope in the second stanza that it is indeed *he* whom Olivia loves, for she writes that she "may command where I adore." Surely she refers to him; he is her steward and is at her command. He reads on and finds that the author of the poem says that because she cannot speak the name of her beloved, that "silence, like a Lucrece knife/ With bloodless stroke my heart doth gore." Such passion thrills Malvolio, but his emotions are stilled by the poem's puzzling last line: "M, O, A, I, doth sway my life." He reasons that "M" *could* stand for "Malvolio," but it should logically be followed by "A," and not by "O." And what of the "I" at the end? Yet the letters could feasibly be pieces of an anagram of his name because his name *does* contain all those letters, albeit in a different sequence.

Then enclosed with the poem, Malvolio discovers a prose letter, which he reads aloud. The author of the letter says that if this letter should, by accident, "fall into [her beloved's] hand," he should be aware that the woman who loves him is, because of the stars (fate) "above" him (meaning that she is socially superior to him), but she begs him not to fear her "greatness." She then states words that have been much-quoted ever since: ". . . some are born great, some achieve greatness, and some have greatness thrust upon 'em." Maria, despite being a mere maid, has done a masterful job of composing exquisite, apologetic modesty, coupled with the tenderness of a love that cannot speak its name.

The author of the love letter continues: Fate beckons to her beloved; he is urged to cast off his usual garments and, instead, he is "commended" to wear yellow stockings, cross-gartered. And, in addition, he should be more "surly with servants"; his tongue should have a 'tang." If he does not do all of these things, he will be thought of as no more than a "steward still" and "not worthy to touch Fortune's fingers." The note is signed with a popular Elizabethan lover's device—an oxymoron: "The Fortunate-Unhappy." The incongruity of combining one mood with its opposite was considered the epitome of epigrammatic wit.

Malvolio is exultant after reading the letter. He vows, as he was "commended," to be *proud* and to *baffle* Sir Toby. To him, there can be no doubt that Olivia wrote the love letter, and if she desires him to wear "yellow stockings . . . cross-gartered," then yellow stockinged and cross-gartered he shall be. His joy is so rapturous that he almost overlooks a postscript: the author is sure that her beloved, if he finds her letter, will recognize himself as her heart's secret treasure; if so, he is to acknowledge his own affection. He is to smile; she repeats the command three times: he is to smile and smile and smile. In other words, Maria is going to make the usually sober and uppity Malvolio look like a grinning fool.

Malvolio exits, and Sir Toby, Sir Andrew, and Fabian emerge from the hedge, just as Maria enters. They are all in excellent spirits. Sir Toby is prepared to marry Maria for her cleverness; he even offers to lie under her and allow her to put her foot upon his neck in the classical position of the victor and the vanquished. She has succeeded beyond all their expectations. Maria says that they won't have long to wait to see the results of their prank. Malvolio is sure to try to see Olivia as soon as possible, and, Maria says, Olivia *detests* yellow stockings, and cross-garters are a fashion which Olivia *abhors*; in addition, Olivia is usually so melancholy about the fact that she cannot choose a husband for herself that Malvolio's endless smiling will drive her into a fury. So off the pranksters go, arm in arm, eagerly anticipating their comic revenge on the officious Malvolio.

Commentary

In contrast to the romantic plot of the preceding scene, we return now to the comic subplot focusing on the duping of Malvolio. This gulling of Malvolio is one of the most comic scenes in the entire play. Sir Toby and Sir Andrew are joined by a new character, Fabian, who has been the victim of Malvolio's sanctimoniousness when he protested to the Lady Olivia that Fabian was involved in the cruel game of "bear baiting," a form of sport in which dogs barked and snapped at a bear chained to a post. As a moral puritan, Malvolio had reported Fabian for "bear baiting" because Olivia disapproved of this cruel sport. Now, however, they hope that this "niggardly rascally sheep-biter" will soon come along, and they will make Malvolio into the "bear" and will "bait" (tease) him.

They intend to fool him "black and blue." Yet, there is no genuine malevolence in their actions. They resent Malvolio's lack of human sympathy and his puritanical arrogance towards them, and furthermore they will use his own arrogant and egotistical nature to play the trick upon him. If he weren't so self-centered and egotistical, it would be impossible to play this trick upon him. Because of this, we find it difficult to sympathize with Malvolio. At this point, Malvolio is like a man who looks down the wrong end of a telescope and sees everything in the world as being diminished in stature.

When Malvolio opens the letter, he thinks that he recognizes Olivia's handwriting; we know, of course, that it is Maria's handwriting. As Malvolio recognizes certain letters, he mouths them aloud; this is a superb comic example of "echo comedy." All through the scene, as Malvolio tries to decipher the letter, the characters in the box-elder hedge continue to make humorous and derogatory remarks. When Malvolio reads in the letter, "If this fall into thy hand, revolve," he turns around on the stage, evoking roars of laughter from those in the box-hedge.

The instructions in the letter will be the source of future comedy; we should remember that Maria conceived the letter knowing full well her mistress's (Lady Olivia's) likes and dislikes. Malvolio is instructed to be surly and distant to the servants, and especially to Olivia's uncle, Sir Toby. Moreover, Malvolio is to wear yellow stockings, an old fashioned symbol of jealousy, already a laughable joke and also a symbol of a low-class serving person; in addition, yellow is a color that Maria knows that the Lady Olivia detests. Malvolio is also to wear the stockings "cross gartered" – that is, he is to wear the garters both above and below the knee, making a cross behind, another custom practiced only by the lowest menials. The irony is that when Malvolio is dressed in this outrageous garb, he hopes to woo a countess! Furthermore, he is to smile continuously at Olivia, and Maria knows that Olivia cannot countenance smiles because she is in "mourning." This is doubly ironic because Malvolio has *never* smiled before; now he will walk around with a foolish smile constantly upon his face.

As a final note, the duping is so perfect that Sir Toby says of Maria: "I could marry this wench for this device" – that is, because of her plan for the duping. When Maria returns, she tells the others to wait until Malvolio first appears before Olivia. He will wear and do everything Olivia detests, and Malvolio's smiling will be so unsuitable to her melancholy disposition that she will probably have him sent away. The comedy lies in the audience's anticipation of this forthcoming scene.

ACT III – SCENE 1

Summary

Viola, disguised as Cesario, has come to plead Orsino's case with Olivia and is now sitting in Olivia's garden, chatting with Feste, Olivia's jester. They play an innocent game of verbal sparring. Their wit is inconsequential, but Cesario cuts it off suddenly, for he tells Feste that while it is pleasant to "dally nicely" with words in harmless punning matches, such duels of wit can easily turn into games of bawdy, "wanton" double entendres. Cesario reminds Feste that Feste is, after all, Olivia's "fool" (another term for jester, but here it is intended to also carry a literal connotation). Feste easily parries Cesario's gentle reprimand. The Lady Olivia, he tells Cesario, has no fool; in fact, she will have no fool "till she be married." Indeed, he is *not* her fool; he is her "corrupter of words." Again, he bests Cesario's own keen wit, while being as "subservient" as possible to the handsome young man; and in this connection, one should note that in this scene, Feste's etiquette of status is ever-present; he prefaces almost every verbal parry between the two with the polite "Sir." Yet there is a good spirit of camaraderie in this scene between the two people. In fact, Feste would enjoy their sparring even more, he says, if Cesario were older and wiser and more worldly; he remarks that it is time that Jove sent Cesario a beard. Viola, forgetting herself momentarily, confesses that she is "almost sick for one" – and then she realizes what she was about to say: she is literally almost *sick* for the love of a man, which of course she can't hope to have as long as she is disguised as a man herself.

At this point, Feste goes in to announce to Olivia that Cesario awaits her in the garden, and while Feste is gone, Viola soliloquizes on the nature of "playing the fool." She recognizes Feste's intelligence; it takes a mature sensitivity to deal with the varying temperaments

and moods of one's superiors while attempting to soothe and entertain them. A jester's wit must be just witty *enough*; he must tread a
thin nimble-witted line, without overstepping social bounds. "Playing the fool," being a jester, Viola says, is "a wise man's art."

While Cesario is waiting, Sir Toby and Sir Andrew enter and
joke with Cesario, but whereas Cesario and Feste entertained the audience with high comedy, Sir Toby and Sir Andrew indulge in low
comedy. Like everyone else (with the exception of Malvolio), both
men are quite impressed with Cesario, especially Sir Andrew, and
much of their joking focuses on their attempting to mimic Cesario's
manners. Summing up Cesario, Sir Andrew comments, "That youth's
a rare courtier."

Olivia and Maria enter, and Olivia quickly dismisses Maria, Uncle Toby, and Sir Andrew so that she can be alone with Cesario. Immediately, she asks for Cesario's hand and then for his name. When
he answers her that he is her servant, she protests: he is Orsino's servant. But, Cesario reminds Olivia, because he is Orsino's servant,
and because his master is *her* servant (because of his love for her),
therefore, he himself is her servant. Olivia is distracted by such logic
and such talk of Orsino. All of her thoughts are on Cesario, and she
would like him to think only of her; as for Orsino, she would prefer
that his mind would be absolutely blank rather than filled with
thoughts of her. She never wants to hear about Orsino again – or his
"suit" (his wooing). She would much prefer that Cesario would present his own "suit" to her – that is, to woo her on his own behalf.

She confesses that the ruse of the forgotten ring and her sending
Malvolio after Cesario was only an excuse; she simply wanted any
excuse to have Cesario return to her. She desperately wants to hear
words of love from him; she begs him to speak. But all Cesario can
reply is that he pities her. Olivia accepts Cesario's rejection with a
certain dignity, but she certainly accepts it with undisguised disap-
pointment. How much better for her, she says, if her heart had cast
her before "a lion" (a nobleman) rather than before "a wolf" (a
servant). She then tells Cesario not to be afraid; she will not press
him any further for love that he cannot give. Yet she cannot but envy
the lucky woman who finally will "harvest" this youth.

Cesario makes ready to go, then he pauses; he asks Olivia one
last time if she has any words for Orsino. She *begs* Cesario to linger:
"Stay," she entreats him, and "prithee, tell me what thou think'st of

me." Cesario and Olivia both confess ambiguously that they are not what they seem, and then Olivia can stand no more. She ends Cesario's adroit evasions of her questions with a passionate declaration of love:

> I love thee, so, that maugre [despite] all thy pride,
> Nor wit nor reason can my passion hide.
>
> (148-49)

Despite this beautiful and spontaneous declaration of love, Cesario of course cannot encourage Olivia, even as a gesture of friendship. He must, in order to maintain his disguise, reject her declarations of love. He tells her, therefore, in the plainest way he can, that he has but "one heart" and that he has given it to "no woman" – nor shall any woman be the "mistress" of that heart, "save I alone." Thus he must bid Olivia adieu; nevermore will he come to speak of his master's love for her. In desperation, Olivia pleads with Cesario: "Come again"; perhaps his heart may yet change and perhaps he may yet come to love her.

Commentary

This scene continues from Act II, Scene 4, when Duke Orsino was preparing to send Cesario on another mission to Olivia. We should still be aware that the scenes have been alternating between the romantic plots and the subplots concerning the gulling of Malvolio. Thus, after the hilarious scene at the end of Act II, Act III opens in Olivia's garden, but the scene is light and jovial because Cesario has just encountered Olivia's Clown, Feste. Together, they delight the audience by turning one another's sentences inside out, demonstrating that each has a finely honed wit.

With the entrance of Sir Toby and Sir Andrew, the punning is continued but, more important, Sir Andrew is able to take note of the manner in which Cesario (Viola) addresses Olivia, which will later give rise to the pretended duel between the two.

After Olivia dismisses everyone in order to be alone with the young messenger, she immediately and desperately wants to hear words of love from Cesario, but all that he can say is that he pities her. Olivia then shows herself to be very much like Duke Orsino –

that is, she is as changeable as the Duke is. At first, she tells Cesario, "I will not have you." Then as Cesario is about to leave, Olivia cannot quite dismiss him before she finds out what he thinks of her: "Stay, I prithee, tell me what thou think'st of me." There follows, then, a series of speeches which serve to remind the audience of the importance and the complications issuing from the fact that everyone is in some sort of disguise:

> *Viola:* That you do think you are not what you are. [That is, that you think that you are in love with a man and you are mistaken.]
>
> *Olivia:* If I think so, I think the same of you. [If I think lower of myself, I think the same of you; i.e., that you are a nobleman in disguise.]
>
> *Viola:* Then think you right: I am not what I am. [She is a girl, not a boy.]
>
> *Olivia:* I would you were as I would have you be. [That is, she wishes that Cesario were a man in love with her.]

After further exchanges, Olivia makes a passionate declaration of love for Cesario:

> Cesario, by the roses of the spring,
> By maidhood, honour, truth and everything. . . .
> I love thee so . . .
> Nor wit nor reason can my passion hide.
>
> (146-49)

Despite this beautiful and spontaneous (and completely unsought) declaration of love, Cesario cannot surrender or explain to Olivia without revealing the disguise; but in refusing her, "he" is guilty in her eyes of wanton cruelty. Lady Olivia is now reduced to the same state as Orsino in this scene. She is pleading for love and is rejected.

ACT III – SCENE 2

Summary

At Olivia's house, Sir Andrew is becoming angry and frustrated. He is making absolutely no progress in winning the affections of

Olivia; he is convinced that she bestows more favors on "the count's serving man" (Cesario) than she does on Sir Andrew. He tells Sir Toby and Fabian that he saw Olivia and Cesario in the orchard, and it was plain to him that Olivia is in love with Cesario. Fabian disagrees; he argues that Olivia is only using Cesario as a ploy to disguise her love for Sir Andrew and thereby make Sir Andrew jealous. Fabian thinks that Sir Andrew should have challenged Cesario on the spot and "banged the youth into dumbness." He laments the fact that Sir Andrew has lost his chance to prove his valor before Olivia's eyes. Now Sir Andrew will "hang like an icicle on a Dutchman's beard" unless he redeems himself by some great and glorious deed. Sir Toby agrees. He proposes that Sir Andrew challenge Cesario to a duel. They themselves will deliver the challenge. Sir Andrew agrees to the plan and goes off to find a pen and some paper, and while he is gone, Sir Toby and Fabian chuckle over the practical joke they have just arranged. They are sure that neither Sir Andrew nor Cesario will actually provoke the other into a real duel.

Maria arrives onstage with the news that Malvolio "does obey every point of the letter." He is sporting yellow stockings; he is cross-gartered, and he "does smile his face into more lines than is in the new map . . . of the Indies."

Commentary

Essentially, this scene serves to advance the subplot, which will culminate when the cowardly Sir Andrew will try to engage Cesario in an actual duel. The first part of this scene reveals that Olivia's love for Cesario is even apparent to someone as dense as Sir Andrew. The mere fact that he has made no progress in his courtship with Olivia does not surprise us. What is astonishing, however, is that he still thinks that he has a chance to win the affection of Olivia. She is obviously far too sensitive and intelligent for this foolish and zany knight, but Sir Andrew is nevertheless jealous of the favors which he has observed Olivia giving to Cesario. To add unity to the scene, we hear that Malvolio is completely following the instructions in the forged letter. Thus, if Sir Andrew is foolish in his belief that he will obtain Olivia's hand, then Malvolio is extremely egotistical to also think so. And as we will see by his dress and demeanor, he will ultimately be revealed as being as foolish as Sir Andrew.

ACT III – SCENE 3

Summary

Sebastian, Viola's twin brother, and Antonio, the sea captain, enter. They are strolling down a street not far from Duke Orsino's palace, and Antonio is explaining that because of his fondness and concern for Sebastian, he simply could not let him wander around Illyria alone, even though he knows that it is risky for him to accompany Sebastian. He knows that he is likely to be arrested on sight if he is recognized, but he had no choice: he likes Sebastian so much that he cannot bear to think of any harm coming to him.

Sebastian is very grateful for the risk which Antonio is taking, and Antonio tells him that it is best that already he should be taking precautions. He asks to be excused so that he can take cover. He gives Sebastian his purse, and they arrange to meet in an hour at a tavern called The Elephant. Thus Sebastian, with a purse full of money in hand, goes off to see the sights of the town.

Commentary

In a comedy dealing essentially with romantic love, this scene continues to investigate another type of love – the manly love that Antonio feels for young Sebastian; he loves young Sebastian enough to follow him into the enemy's country, where he himself is in danger of being arrested and severely punished if he is discovered. But it is not merely love that Antonio feels for Sebastian; it is also jealousy, for Antonio says:

> And not all love to see you, though so much
> As might have drawn one to a longer voyage,
> But jealousy what might befall your travel.
>
> (6-8)

The trust and affection that Antonio has for Sebastian is also seen at the end of the scene when Antonio gives his purse of money to Sebastian in case the young man wants to purchase something. This gift of money will later become an important part of the plot when Viola, dressed as Cesario, is mistaken by Antonio for Sebastian. Thus, another purpose of the scene is to bring Sebastian into the same city where Viola is, thus setting the stage for further complications involving mistaken identities. The plot is rapidly reaching the point of complication where Shakespeare will have to begin unraveling it.

ACT III – SCENE 4

Summary

Olivia and Maria are in the garden, and Olivia is making plans to entertain Cesario; she sent him an invitation, and he has promised to come to visit her. She is very excited at the prospect and wonders how to treat him, how to "feast him." She is afraid that he will think that she is trying to "buy" him. Where is Malvolio, she wonders; he is usually grave and polite and can be counted on to calm her nerves.

Smiling foolishly, Malvolio enters. His whole appearance has changed since we last saw him; his dark clothes are gone, as is his dour appearance. Maria's forged love note has changed him from being "sad and civil" into being a merrily smiling fabrication of a courtier; he complains a bit about the cross-gartering causing "some obstruction in the blood," but he suffers gladly – if it will please Olivia. Smiling again and again, he kisses his hand and blows his kisses toward Olivia. She is dumbfounded by his unexplainable, incongruous dress and behavior, but Malvolio doesn't seem to notice. He prances before her, quoting various lines of the letter which he supposes that Olivia wrote to him, and in particular, he dwells on the "greatness" passage. Olivia tries to interrupt what he is saying, but to no avail; he rambles on and on until she is convinced that he must be suffering from "midsummer madness."

A servant announces the arrival of Cesario, and Olivia places the "mad" Malvolio in Maria's charge; in fact, she suggests that the whole household staff should look after him. Meanwhile, Malvolio, remembering the orders which Maria inserted into the letter, spurns Maria, is hostile to Sir Toby, and is insulting to Fabian. He finally drives them all to exasperation and fury, and when he leaves, they make plans to lock him up in a dark room, a common solution for handling a lunatic in Elizabethan days. Olivia won't mind, says Sir Toby: "My niece is already in the belief that he's mad."

Sir Andrew enters, and he carries a copy of his challenge to Cesario. He is exceedingly proud of the language, which, we discover as Sir Toby reads it aloud, is exceedingly stilted and obtuse and, in short, is exceedingly ridiculous. Sir Andrew's spirits are high, and Maria decides that the time is ripe for more fun: she tells him that Cesario is inside with Olivia. Sir Toby adds that now is the time to corner the lad and as soon as he sees him, he should draw his sword and "swear horrible." According to Sir Toby, "a terrible oath, with a swaggering accent sharply twanged off, gives manhood." Offering his services, Sir Toby says that he will deliver Sir Andrew's challenge "by word of mouth." (He is sure that Cesario, clever young man that he is, will instantly see the harmless humor in the absurdly worded challenge; it couldn't possibly "breed . . . terror in the youth." And thus the practical jokers exit—just as Olivia and Cesario enter.

This scene-within-a-scene is very much like ones we have already witnessed: Cesario pleads that his master, Duke Orsino, should be considered a serious suitor, and Olivia changes the subject to Cesario himself, as she gives him a diamond brooch containing a miniature portrait of herself. Cesario accepts it politely and courteously, and Olivia exits.

Sir Toby and Fabian enter and stop Cesario before he can leave for Orsino's palace. Sir Toby tells Cesario that Sir Andrew, his "interceptor," is waiting for him and is ready to challenge him to a sword fight. Cesario panics (remember that he is Viola, who knows nothing of violence and dueling). Sir Toby continues: Sir Andrew is a "devil in a private brawl," for he has killed three men already ("souls and bodies hath he divorced three"). Cesario, says Sir Toby, can do only one thing to defend himself against Sir Andrew: "strip your sword stark naked." Such advice is alarming. Cesario begs Sir Toby to seek out this knight and find out what offense he has committed, and so Sir Toby exits, ostensibly to go on his assigned errand, leaving Cesario in the company of Signior, a title Sir Toby impromptly bestowed on Fabian, all in the spirit of their practical joking. These two exit then, just as Sir Toby and Sir Andrew enter.

Sir Toby describes in vivid, violent language Cesario's fierceness. Sir Andrew quakes: "I'll not meddle with him"; he is even willing to give Cesario his horse, "grey Capilet," to avoid the duel. Fabian and Cesario return, and Sir Toby taunts both Cesario and Sir Andrew into drawing their swords, all the while assuring them that no real harm will come to either of them.

At this point, a true swordsman enters. It is Antonio, and mistaking young Cesario for Sebastian, he tells Sir Andrew to put up his sword—unless he wants to fight Antonio. Sir Toby draws his sword and is ready to take on Antonio when a troop of officers enters. Antonio has been recognized on the streets, and Orsino has sent out his men to arrest him. Dejectedly, Antonio turns to Cesario (who he believes to be Sebastian). He asks him for his purse back, and when Cesario naturally denies having ever received it, the sea captain is both saddened and enraged by this apparent ingratitude. He denounces this youth, "this god," whom he "snatched . . . out of the jaws of death . . . [and offered the] "sanctity of love." "Sebastian," he tells Cesario, "thou . . . virtue is beauty, but the beauteous-evil/ Are empty trunks o'erflourished by the devil."

As the officers lead Antonio away, Viola is almost ready to believe what *may* be possible: Sebastian *may* be alive! It is possible that this man saved her twin brother, Sebastian, and Antonio may have just now confused her with Sebastian because of her disguise. Breathlessly, she prays that "imagination [should] prove true/ That I, dear brother, be now ta'en for you." Viola exits, and unwilling to miss their fun, Sir Toby and Fabian easily convince old Sir Andrew that Cesario is a coward, and the three of them set out after Orsino's page.

Commentary

This scene is not only the longest scene in the entire play, it is also longer than the entirety of Act IV and the entirety of Act V. Likewise, there are many divisions within this scene in terms of several different groupings of characters on the stage and several uses of mistaken identities. Malvolio is mistaken for a madman by Olivia, Olivia is mistaken for a true love by Malvolio, Viola is mistaken for a man who allegedly insulted Sir Andrew, Viola is mistaken for a man with a "heart of stone" by Lady Olivia, and Viola is mistaken for her brother Sebastian by Antonio.

Before Malvolio arrives, Maria warns Olivia (and the audience) that Malvolio is "possessed," that he is out of his mind and that his sanity has been taken over (possessed) by devils. When Malvolio does appear, we are not disappointed. As in other scenes in *Twelfth Night*, the staging is an extremely important part of the total effect. As Maria goes out and returns, ushering in Malvolio, the change in the steward is dramatic. Instead of being "sad and civil," he smiles broadly and continually; he kisses his hand to the Lady Olivia, and instead of being dressed in sober black, he is in yellow stockings with tight cross-garters in a contrasting color. Malvolio keeps on referring to various lines of the letter which he supposes that Olivia wrote to him, but since Olivia did not write the letter, she has no idea what he is talking about. Furthermore, Olivia does not realize that Malvolio is *quoting*; she assumes his talk to be the ravings of a madman, and she wishes that he would leave her sight and be treated for his madness.

Meanwhile, on the stage, the only one present who does know what Malvolio is referring to is Maria, who is probably behind Malvolio laughing uproariously. Knowing the contents of the letter (since she wrote it), Maria very cunningly asks Malvolio some questions that cause him to continue quoting from the letter; this, of course, heightens the impression that he is raving.

As Malvolio insists on quoting line by line from the letter, and as he returns time after time to the "greatness" passage, Olivia becomes more and more confused, for she thinks that he is madly rambling. Finally, feeling compassion for her steward, she thinks that "this is very midsummer madness."

Sir Toby's delight in practical jokes is again illustrated as he plans some good sport between Sir Andrew and Cesario (Viola). He is, of course, working always under the assumption that no harm will come to either party since the challenge and his arrangements will "so fright them both that they will kill one another by the look, like cockatrices." Sir Toby, of course, is right. The duel between Sir Andrew Aguecheek and Cesario (Viola) is one of the high points of the comedy of this play. Equally absurd is the fact that the pretended duel is fought over Lady Olivia, whom Cesario (Viola) has rejected and who is not even aware of the foolish Sir Andrew's intentions. In fact, part of the high comedy involves the egotistical absurdity of Malvolio's thinking that the high-born Lady Olivia would stoop to love him and, in addition, the foolishness of Sir Andrew's thinking that he has enough of a romantic chance with this lady to enter into a duel upon her behalf. The absurdity of Sir Andrew's and Cesario's dueling for the love of Olivia is one of the most ludicrous duels in the history of the stage. Then to add to the absurdity, Antonio comes on stage to defend "Sebastian" (Viola disguised as Cesario) and finds himself dueling with the fat, belching Sir Toby.

The various elements of the plot are slowly being brought together. Viola now realizes that she has been mistaken for her
brother, thereby preparing the way for Sebastian to be mistaken for
her by the Lady Olivia.

ACT IV – SCENE 1

Summary

The scene opens on the street in front of Olivia's house. Sebastian
and Feste are talking, and we realize that Feste has mistaken Sebastian for Cesario. Feste *insists* that his mistress has sent Feste to *him*,
meaning Cesario. Sebastian is annoyed at the jester's persistence;
"Thou art a foolish fellow," he says, and gives him a generous tip to
send him on his way – or else he will give Feste "worse payment,"
meaning a kick in the rump if he doesn't leave him in peace.

Sir Andrew, Sir Toby, and Fabian enter, and Sir Andrew
assumes that Sebastian is the "cowardly" Cesario; Sir Andrew strikes
him, whereupon Sebastian promptly beats Sir Andrew, asking, "Are
all the people mad?" Feste says that he is going to report to Olivia all
that has happened, and she will *not* be pleased to learn that her
favorite suitor, the reluctant Cesario, has quarreled with Olivia's uncle and with Sir Andrew. Sir Toby, meanwhile, decides that it is time
for him to act; he grabs the young upstart (Sebastian) by the hand in
an effort to save Sir Andrew from greater injury.

Olivia arrives, assumes that Sebastian is Cesario, and pleads
with him to go into the house. She severely reprimands Sir Toby and
sends him away, out of her sight, and he exits, taking the other two
with him. She apologizes for the "pranks of [these] ruffians," and
while she is talking, Sebastian is speechless. He cannot believe what
is happening: he is being wooed in the most ardent of terms by a
beautiful young countess; if this be a dream, he says, "let fancy still
my sense in Lethe . . . let me sleep." Olivia is insistent: "Come, I
prithee," she says, and begs him to marry her. Without hesitation,
Sebastian accepts: "Madame, I will," he says, and off they dash to
look for a priest to perform the ceremony.

Commentary

This scene begins by re-emphasizing the comic ramifications in-
herent in the various mistaken identities and disguises. Feste has

been sent by Olivia to Cesario (Viola) to deliver a message, but he delivers it to Sebastian, because Viola's twin brother looks exactly like her. Thus this is the first case of a very natural and very understandable case of mistaken identity; the comedy here lies in the fact that Sebastian does not know what Feste is talking about, and Feste feels that "Nothing that is so is so." They talk at cross purposes, and we (the audience) know why. This is yet another case of dramatic irony used for a delightful comic effect.

Even more comic, however, is the fact that Sir Andrew, an innate coward, is convinced that Cesario (Viola) is frightened of him—which is actually true. However, *this* man is Sebastian, and thus this is a completely different matter. Consequently, when Sir Andrew begins striking Sebastian, Sebastian returns the blows double-fold until Sir Toby has to restrain Sebastian. Again, the comedy here derives in large part from the stage action coupled with the comedy of mistaken identities—a theme that is now almost absurd.

When Olivia arrives and discovers her uncle physically "man handling" Sebastian, whom she thinks is Cesario, her anger at her uncle will affect the comic subplot against Malvolio because Sir Toby will be out of favor with his niece and will no longer feel the freedom to torment her steward.

By the time that Sebastian has been mistaken by Feste, then beaten by Sir Andrew, then restrained by Sir Toby, and then addressed in terms of soothing and passionate love by a beautiful noble lady, whom he has never seen, the youth is ready to believe that he is in the strangest country of the world, or else he has gone mad. In contrast, Olivia is delighted at the sudden turn of events; she believes that Cesario (Viola) finally loves her.

ACT IV—SCENE 2

Summary

In order to fully appreciate this scene, you should recall that Olivia gave Sir Toby and the household staff orders to take care of Malvolio and the "midsummer madness" that turned him into a grinning zany, tightly cross-gartered, and garbed in yellow stockings. They locked him in a dark room, and now Maria and Feste prepare to pull a few more pranks on the supercilious, overbearing Malvolio. Feste disguises himself as a parson and plans to make a "mercy call" on the "poor mad prisoner." He will assume the role of Sir Topas, the curate. The interview is a masterpiece of low, broad comedy.

Feste, as Sir Topas, knows just enough Latin phrases to lace them into his interview, along with pedantic nonsense and pseudo-metaphysical drivel concerning the philosophy of existence. The imprisoned steward, of course, is extremely relieved to hear what he believes to be the parson's voice, for he fondly imagines that his deliverance from this darkened room of a prison is near. This is not the case, however; he will "remain in his darkness" for some time to come.

When Feste slips out for a moment, Sir Toby suggests that Feste use his natural voice to speak with Malvolio; things have taken a turn for the worse, and he wants to release Malvolio and end this charade. He is afraid that Olivia might turn him out of the house, and he "cannot pursue with any safety this sport to the upshot."

Feste is having too much fun, though, to pay much attention to Toby's fears; he enters Malvolio's room, assumes his ecclesiastical voice, and tries to convince the steward that there are two visitors in the room instead of one. Malvolio pleads that he is *not* insane, and finally Feste is persuaded to bring Malvolio some ink, a pen, and some writing paper so that he can "set down to [his] lady" proof of his sanity.

Commentary

Once again, disguise is used to create comic effect. This time, Feste disguises himself as a parson and appears before Malvolio. The disguise utilizes a black gown, the same type of gown that Malvolio had worn earlier. The comedy is multifold: Malvolio thinks that with the appearance of the parson some light will be shed upon his insanity, but actually, Malvolio will have to remain in darkness for some time to come. As Feste says: "There is no darkness but ignorance," and certainly Malvolio was ignorant to think that Olivia could ever be attracted to him.

ACT IV – SCENE 3

Summary

Sitting in Olivia's garden, Sebastian is enjoying the bliss of being loved by a beautiful and rich countess, although he is still thoroughly confused about *why* all this has happened to him. As he sits alone, he admires the lovely pearl which Olivia has given to him, and he wonders why Antonio did not meet him at The Elephant Inn, where they had agreed to meet. All of this seems truly like a dream; yet, looking at the pearl, he holds tangible proof that this is not a dream at all. He wishes that Antonio were with him to advise him; he heard that the sea captain did stay at the inn. Yet where is he now? And he wonders if the beautiful Olivia is mad – and, of course, there is another possibility: perhaps he himself is mad.

Olivia enters with a priest and tells Sebastian that she wants him to accompany her and the priest "into the chantry" (a private chapel). There, "before him/ And underneath that consecrated roof," Sebastian will "plight [Olivia] the fullest assurance of [his] faith." Sebastian agrees to marry Olivia; the marriage will be kept secret until later, when they will have a splendid, public ceremony, befitting Olivia's rank. They exit, arm in arm, for the private ceremony, as the fourth act comes to a close.

Commentary

The audience can readily sympathize with Sebastian's confusion and astonishment over the course of events that have taken place, and at the same time they can vicariously experience the great bliss of being loved. Sebastian tries to question reality, but he looks at the pearl that has been given him, and we must remember that Olivia is a person of great beauty; one could easily fall in love with her on first sight. For some modern critics, Sebastian's love for Olivia might strain one's belief, but we must remember that this is a romantic comedy, set in faraway Illyria, and Sebastian himself questions the plausibility of the events. The mistaken identities are, of course, a stock element of romantic comedies, and the forthcoming marriage between Olivia and Sebastian will provide the basis for all of the complications that will be unraveled in the next act.

ACT V – SCENE 1

Summary

This last act, which consists of only a single scene, takes place on a street in front of Olivia's house. Feste is reluctantly carrying

Malvolio's letter to Olivia (pleading Malvolio's sanity), but Fabian is trying to discourage him from reading it. Feste, needless to say, is in no great hurry to deliver it.

Duke Orsino, Cesario (Viola), Curio, and others enter, and Orsino has a few words with Feste; he is pleased with Feste's quick wit and gives him a gold coin and tells him to announce to Olivia that he is here to speak with her and, furthermore, to "bring her along"; if he does, there may be more gold coins for Feste.

Cesario (Viola) sees Antonio approaching with several officers and tells Orsino that this is the man who rescued him from Sir Andrew earlier. (Antonio, of course, is still under arrest). Orsino remembers Antonio well; when he last saw Antonio, the sea captain's face was "besmeared/ As black as Vulcan in the smoke of war." Antonio was the captain of a pirate ship then and did great damage to Orsino's fleet. Yet despite their past differences, Orsino remembers Antonio as being a brave and honorable opponent.

When he is asked to explain how he happened to be in Illyria, Antonio explains to Orsino that he is the victim of "witchcraft" — that is, he saved Cesario's life, and then this "most ingrateful boy" would not return the purse of money which he lent him earlier.

At this instant, Olivia makes a grand entrance with her attendants. When Orsino sees Olivia entering, he says that "heaven walks on earth." He tells himself that "this youth" (Cesario) "hath tended" him for three months; Antonio's words, of course, are impossible.

Olivia's ire is rankled. She asks Orsino what he wants — other than what he can't have — and she accuses Cesario of breaking an appointment with her. Frustrated to the point of madness himself, Orsino turns on Cesario: it is all his fault that Olivia has rejected him, and he will have his revenge. He knows that Olivia loves Cesario, and he is ready to "tear out [Cesario from Olivia's] cruel eye" for bestowing all her loving glances at Cesario. He orders Cesario to come with him for his "thoughts are ripe in mischief." Even though he values Cesario very much, yet he will "sacrifice the lamb . . . to spite a raven's heart." Olivia is appalled: where is the haughty Orsino taking her new husband? Cesario replies that he goes with Orsino willingly; he would, for Orsino, "a thousand deaths die." He says that he loves Orsino "more than I love these eyes, more than my life . . . [and] all the more, than e'er I shall love wife."

Olivia is thunderstruck: "Me, detested! how am I beguiled!" She calls for the priest who married her to Cesario (in fact, to Sebastian), and the priest enters and attests to the fact that a marriage did indeed take place between these two young people.

Now it is *Orsino* who is furious. This "proxy," this young messenger whom he hired to carry letters of love to Olivia, hoodwinked him and married Olivia himself. He turns to this "dissembling cub" and tells him to "take her; but direct thy feet/ Where thou and I henceforth may never meet." Cesario (Viola) attempts to protest, but Olivia hushes him: "Oh, do not fear . . . thou hast too much fear."

Suddenly, Sir Andrew enters, crying loudly for a surgeon; Sir Toby also needs one. They say that they have been wounded by Cesario (Sebastian), and Sir Andrew's head is broken and Sir Toby has a "bloody coxcomb." They point their finger to Cesario (Viola): "Here he is!" Cesario (Viola) protests once more. He has hurt no one; yet it is true that Sir Andrew drew his sword and challenged him once to a duel, but certainly Cesario (Viola) never harmed Sir Andrew.

It seems that the surgeon is drunk and cannot come, and although Olivia tries to find out who is responsible for this bloody business, she cannot, for confusion reigns as Sir Toby and Sir Andrew help one another off to bed.

The key to the solution of all of this confusion now enters: it is *Sebastian*. He apologizes to Olivia for having injured Sir Toby. Orsino is the first to express astonishment at the identical appearance of Sebastian and Cesario. It is almost impossible to distinguish between them, except by the colors of their clothes. Sebastian then reminds Olivia of the words which they exchanged only a short time ago, and he calls her his "sweet one." He joyfully recognizes Antonio and confesses how "the hours [have] racked and tortured" him since he lost him. Like Orsino, Antonio is amazed. He compares Cesario and Sebastian to "an apple, cleft in two." Viola (Cesario) begins to speak then; she tells Sebastian that he is very much like a twin brother who she fears perished in a "watery tomb." Her father was Sebastion; he had a mole on one brow – and at this point, Sebastian interrupts her: so did *his* father. Moreover, both agree that this man died when they were thirteen years old.

Viola then reveals that her real identity is hidden by "masculine usurp'd attire"; she is Sebastian's lost twin sister, and she can prove it by taking them to the home of a sea captain who knows of her disguise and is keeping her women's clothes for her; however they must produce Malvolio because he has been holding the sea captain imprisoned.

Sebastian turns to Olivia and tells her that she has been "mistook." Had she married Cesario (Viola), she would "have been contracted to a maid." But he gives her good news also. As her husband, he is a bit of a "maid" himself – that is, he is a virgin ("both maid and man"). Olivia calls immediately for Malvolio; she wants to hear why he has had this sea captain imprisoned, and she asks that he be specifically brought before her, even though "they say, poor gentleman, he's much distract."

At this point, Feste enters with Malvolio's letter, written as proof of his sanity. Olivia tells him to read it aloud, and he does, in an affected voice that makes everyone laugh. Olivia then gives the letter to Fabian to read. She is not truly convinced that Malvolio is all that mad. When he enters, he brings Maria's "love note" with him. Olivia instantly recognizes the handwriting as being Maria's. Thus she begins to reconstruct the intricacies of the practical joke that her servants have played on Malvolio. She declares that Malvolio shall be both plaintiff and judge of his own case against the pranksters.

Recounting all of the secret plottings which have taken place, Fabian confesses his and Sir Toby's roles in their attempt to take revenge on Malvolio. He also confesses that it was Sir Toby who persuaded Maria to write the forged love note, and that, "in recompense," he has married her. Olivia expresses pity for Malvolio; he has been "most notoriously abused," and then in lines of stately blank verse, Count Orsino ends the play by turning to Viola and telling her that while she seemed very dear to him once as a man, she is now his "mistress and fancy queen." Everyone exits, and Feste is left onstage.

He sings one last song, one of the most philosophical jester's songs in all of Shakespeare's plays. It tells of the development of men, focusing on the various stages of their lives, and putting all of the serious matters of the life of men into the dramatic context of this comedy – whose purpose is, after all, only to "please."

Commentary

Unlike the earlier acts which were divided into several individual scenes, this final act has only one scene. This gives a heightened sense of unity because most of the diverse plots, themes, complications, and mistaken identities must be unraveled and resolved. However, there are a few minor details that are left unresolved. For example, Antonio had earlier feared that he would be arrested, and we are never to know why. In this scene, Antonio is also accused of being a pirate and a sea thief and also as someone who attacked Duke Orsino's fleet, causing great damage; yet Antonio denies he was ever a thief or a pirate, and even those accusing him (Orsino, for example) admit that he has always conducted himself in honorable and heroic fashion. Whatever the cause of the conflict between Antonio and Orsino, it is left unclear. Likewise, why Malvolio has Viola's sea captain imprisoned and awaiting trial is a total mystery; this is a matter which is also left unresolved.

The first interchange of wit in the first part of the act between Duke Orsino and Feste the Clown introduces the first resolution of the various complications in the play; Feste is on his way to Olivia with a letter from Malvolio which will clear up the plot concerning the gulling and "imprisoning" of Malvolio. With the entrance of the arrested Antonio, however, confusion mounts to a higher crescendo as Cesario (Viola) is first accused of bewitching and then betraying Antonio; then there is an accusation made of his alienating Olivia's affections from Orsino; and third, Cesario (Viola) is accused of betraying the bond of marriage entered into with Olivia and attested to by the priest.

Cesario (Viola) is left speechless, of course, when these accusations are made. Antonio's charge is denied by Orsino; he knows for a fact that Cesario has been in his service for three months (events have transpired so fast that Shakespeare realized that his audience might not be aware that three months have really elapsed; thus he has Orsino point out the fact here).

The priest's testimony discredits Cesario's relationship with Orsino; thus Orsino threatens to play the role of the tyrant; that is, he will punish Olivia by putting her love, Cesario, to death—in spite of his own strong attraction to the youth. The sudden appearance of Sir Andrew, followed by Sir Toby, creates another diversion. They enter wounded, calling loudly for a "surgeon," and accuse Cesario of having beaten them violently; clearly, we *can* see that they have indeed been beaten by *someone*. But the description of their assailant as a very fierce devil scarcely fits our knowledge of the character of the gentle young Cesario (Viola), even though their bleeding heads confirm a beating.

When Sebastian enters, the final solution of the puzzle is now at hand. The most striking thing about him is his close physical resemblance to Cesario; remember that he and his sister are both dressed as men; it is almost impossible to distinguish between them, except by the colors of their clothes. But because Viola recognizes her brother, the attention of this final scene is on Sebastian, who gradually comes to recognize that the youth dressed as Cesario is really Viola. In this recognition scene, then, all parties are happily joined to each other, even though we do not see Sir Toby and Maria, who have just been married, according to Feste.

Malvolio is the only person left disgruntled. There is no humor, no charity, and no forgiveness in him, and after his departure, the play ends on a happy note, with the promise of happiness for almost everyone.

CHARACTER ANALYSES

Viola

For most critics, Viola is one of Shakespeare's most delightful and beloved feminine creations from his comedies. Surrounded by characters who express the extremes of emotionalism and melancholy—that is, Viola is caught between Duke Orsino's extreme melancholy and Lady Olivia's aggressive emotionalism—yet she represents the norm of behavior in this strange world of Illyria.

Due to her circumstances, she is, first of all, a very practical and resourceful person. As a shipwrecked orphan who has no one to protect her, she must resort to some means whereby her safety is assured. She knows that a single woman unattended in a foreign land would be in an extremely dangerous position. Consequently, she evaluates the sea captain's character, finds it suitable, and wisely places her trust in him; then she disguises herself as a boy so that she will be safe and have a man's freedom to move about without protection. Consequently, Viola is immediately seen to be quick-witted enough to evaluate her situation, of sound enough judgment to recognize the captain's integrity, resourceful enough to conceive of the disguise, and practical enough to carry out this design.

Viola also has a native intelligence, an engaging wit, and an immense amount of charm. These are the qualities which will help her obtain her position with Duke Orsino, and they are also the same qualities which cause Lady Olivia to immediately fall in love with her. It was her charming personality, we should remember, which won her the sea captain's loyalty, without whose help her disguise would have never succeeded. And within a short three days' time, her wit, charm, loyalty, and her skill in music and conversation won for her the complete trust of Duke Orsino. We should also remember that even though she is in love with the Duke, she is loyal in her missions when she tries to win Lady Olivia's love for him.

For the modern audience, Viola's charm lies in her simple, straightforward, good-humored personality. She could have used her disguise for all sorts of connivings, yet she is forthright and honest in all of her dealings with Lady Olivia and with Duke Orsino, albeit she does use her disguise to entertain the audience with delightful verbal puns. Perhaps the most surprising thing about Viola is that a young lady in possession of so many attributes falls in love with someone who is as moody and changeable as the Duke.

Olivia

The Comedy opens with music being played to remind the Duke of Olivia; the first scene discusses the lady's charms; and she is mentioned in the second scene as having lost a brother. Viola feels an instant empathy with a person mourning a lost brother since she herself believes that her brother is also drowned. In the third scene, Olivia's house is the setting, and in the fourth scene, Olivia is again the central subject of discussion. Thus, we hear a great deal about this important lady before we actually meet her.

At first, Olivia seems to be the emotional counterpart for the Duke; he is a melancholy parallel for Olivia, and Olivia has sworn to abjure the world for seven years to mourn for her dead brother, an act of extreme sentimental melancholy. Olivia is also the opposite of Viola in many ways. While Olivia is attracted to her opposite (Viola in the guise of Cesario), Viola will be attracted to her opposite, Duke Orsino.

Other than the melodramatic pose that Olivia is assuming at the beginning of the play (we know it to be a pose because she is willing to immediately discard it in order to flirt with Cesario), Olivia is presented as being essentially an intelligent woman with a number of good qualities. Her intelligence is constantly seen in the many household matters that she has to attend to. She has to contend with her drunken uncle, Sir Toby Belch, and when Malvolio presents himself in his mad garb, she feels compassion for her foolish steward.

Yet, earler when Feste made fun of Malvolio, the over-serious steward, Olivia was fully capable of appreciating the Clown's wit.

The single quality that characterizes Olivia best is perhaps her impetuous love and her assertion of it. She is much more aggressive in the pursuit of her love than is Duke Orsino in his pursuit of Olivia. While she recognizes the Duke's good qualities and acknowledges them, she is adamant in her refusals, and, thus, it is part of the comedy that the lady who has no sympathy for the Duke falls so irrationally in love with a young girl disguised as a young boy. When she discovers that she has actually married young Sebastian, Viola's twin, she quickly transfers her love to him, just as Duke Orsino is able to transfer his love to Viola.

Duke Orsino

The Duke is basically characterized by the first line that he utters — "If music be the food of love, play on" — that is, he is the most (or one of the most) melancholy characters that Shakespeare ever created. His entire opening speech is filled with words such as "excess," "surfeiting," "appetite . . . sickening," and "dying fall," words which show the Duke to be sentimentally in love with love. He has seen Olivia, and the very sight of her has fascinated him to such an extent that his romantic imagination convinces him that he will perish if she does not consent to be his wife. Thus, this romantic, melancholy indulgence is the crux of the play because the Duke uses Cesario (Viola) as his emissary to court Olivia.

The Duke, however, is as changeable as the "sea" and as inconsistant as "an opal in the sunlight." His languid craving for music is equated by his languid reclining upon an opulent couch and his requesting attention, and then suddenly becoming bored by what he has just requested. It is, however, the Duke's changeable nature which allows us to believe that he can immediately switch his love for Olivia to Viola at the end of the play.

The Duke is, however, according to Olivia and others, a perfect gentleman. He is handsome, brave, courtly, virtuous, noble, wealthy, gracious, loyal and devoted — in short, he is everything a young lady could wish for in a husband. This is ultimately what makes it believeable that Viola does fall in love with him immediately.

Sir Toby Belch, Sir Andrew Aguecheek, and Maria

The two male comic characters, while considered as a sort of team, represent the opposite sides of a coin. Sir Toby Belch, as his name indicates, is earthy, crude, very fat, and jolly. Sir Andrew Aguecheek, as his name might indicate, is tall, long, thin, and balding.

Sir Toby is also the opposite to Sir Andrew in intellect. Sir Toby is actually a sharp, witty person who, even when he is drunk, is capable of making a good pun or of creating an ingenious and humorous plot complication. For example, he appreciates Maria not for her looks or for romantic matters, but because she is capable of contriving such a good joke against Malvolio. We are not surprised, at the end of the play, when he marries her.

Sir Toby's character is based upon an earlier comic character of Shakespeare's, Sir John Falstaff. Both characters share many of the same qualities. For example, both of them are given to excessive drinking and eating, both love a good prank, and both enjoy harassing serious-minded people like Malvolio. Thus, while Sir Toby is a knight, he is still a rather corrupt individual. After all, the only reason he keeps Sir Andrew Aguecheek around is to gull him out of his money. The fact that he can tease and play jokes on Sir Andrew is secondary to his primary purpose of using Sir Andrew's money to continue drinking. He is indeed guilty of misusing his niece's house and of abusing her servants; yet in spite of all of his faults, Sir Toby is, perhaps, Shakespeare's most delightful comic creation, after Sir John Falstaff.

Sir Andrew Aguecheek, on the other hand, is merely a foolish fellow who is easily gulled and who does not realize that he has been cheated. It would take a very foolish fellow to think that such a rich and beautiful lady as Olivia would seriously consider this "ague"-looking, skinny, balding, and ugly man as a possible suitor. In addition, he is a coward, and a good deal of the humor surrounding him comes from how he is tricked into fighting with Cesario, and then later, what happens when he encounters Sebastian. Sir Toby sums up this comical knight with the comment: he is "an ass-head, and a coxcomb, and a knave; a thin-faced knave, a gull."

William Hazlitt, a famous Romantic writer of the early 1800s, wrote charmingly of these marvelous comic characters; he was delighted by their contrasting characters. Sir Toby was sanguine, red-nosed, burly, a practical joker, and always ready for "a hair of the dog that bit him." He is a fitting opposite to Sir Andrew (pale as though he had the ague), with thin, smooth, straw-colored hair. Hazlitt was deeply amused by this wretched little nincompoop who values himself on his dancing and fencing, being quarrelsome yet chicken-hearted, boastful and yet timid in the same breath, and grotesque in every movement. Sir Andrew is a mere echo and shadow of the heroes of his admiration, born to be the sport of his associates, their puppet, and the butt of their jokes; and while he is so brainless as to think it possible he may win the love of the beautiful Olivia, he has at the same time an inward suspicion of his own stupidity which now and then comes in refreshingly: "Methinks sometimes I have no more wit than a Christian or an ordinary man has; but I am a great eater of beef, and, I believe, that does harm to my wit." He often does not understand the simplest word he hears, and he is such a mere reflex and a parrot that "I too" is, as it were, the watchword of his existence. Sir Toby sums him up in the phrase: "For Andrew, if he were opened, and you find so much blood in his liver as will clog the foot of a flea, I'll eat the rest of the anatomy."

And of Maria, Hazlitt writes: "We have a sneaking kindness for Maria and her rogueries. She fits in with Sir Toby Belch's view of the world, and it is true that this 'youngest wren of nine' and 'as pretty a piece of Eve's flesh as any in Illyria' later married him. They are both opposed to Malvolio, because they represent the 'cakes and ale' of which, because he was a virtuous puritan, Malvolio so disapproved."

Malvolio

Malvolio's function in this comedy is more difficult to evaluate. Certainly, on a basic level, he functions as a contrast to the merry-makers, Sir Toby and Sir Andrew; he is a somber shadow of the aristocratic world and a sober reminder to Feste that the world is a serious place. While the other characters are almost always happy, Malvolio is grave. He emphasizes the importance of dignity, decency, decorum and "good order"; yet when he thinks he sees a chance for advancement with Olivia, he abandons all such proper conduct and behaves like an utter fool.

Early in the play, Maria characterizes him as a puritan. He is always dressed in the black, puritanical costume of the puritan of that time – a person whom most people in this play would despise. Yet he is respected by Olivia, and she does wish to retain his good services.

It is Malvolio's ultimate egotism which makes him an easy prey for the pranksters. Before they leave the forged, fake letter from Olivia for him, he is walking in the garden, daydreaming about the pleasures and the powers he would have if he were married to Olivia. Thus, his own sense of conceit makes him an easy dupe for the trick that is played upon him. Even though the ruse is rather harsh, yet the audience dislikes anyone so opposed to having a good time and yet, hypocritically, he tries to imagine himself as the harsh guardian over Sir Toby after he successfully woos and marries Lady Olivia.

QUESTIONS FOR REVIEW

1. This play is based on a series of mistaken identities and disguises of one sort or another. Identify as many of the disguises as you can and explain how each of them functions in the plot development.

2. Describe the nature and type of love to which Duke Orsino is an easy prey.

3. Why does Duke Orsino use Cesario (Viola) to woo Olivia? Why doesn't he court her himself? Is it significant that they meet only once in the play and that this meeting is at the very end of the comedy? If so, why?

4. What qualities does Duke Orsino possess that allow Viola to fall in love with him?

5. Discuss Viola's use of her disguise.

6. Discuss the various changes that Lady Olivia undergoes during the course of the play and how can they be accounted for.

7. Relate the comic subplots dealing with Sir Andrew's and Malvolio's love for Lady Olivia to the main romantic plots.

8. How many separate plots are there? How can each be related to the other?

9. How does music function in this Comedy?

10. How is Feste the Clown related to both the comic and the romantic plots?

SELECTED BIBLIOGRAPHY

ADAMS, J. Q. *A Life of William Shakespeare.* Boston: Houghton Mifflin Co., 1923.

ALEXANDER, PETER. *Shakespeare.* Oxford: Oxford University Press, 1964.

BEVINGTON, DAVID. *Shakespeare.* Arlington Heights, Ill.: A.H.M. Publications, 1978.

BLOOM, EDWARD A., ed. *Shakespeare 1564-1964.* Providence: Brown University Press, 1964.

GIBSON, H. N. *The Shakespeare Claimants.* New York: Barnes & Noble, Inc., 1962.

HEILMAN, ROBERT B. *Magic in the Web.* Lexington, Kentucky: University of Kentucky Press, 1956.

HAYLES, N. K. "Sexual Disguise in *As You Like It* and *Twelfth Night, Shakespeare Survey,* Vol. 32, pp. 63-72, 1978.

HIBBARD, G. R. "Love, Marriage and Money in Shakespeare's Theatre and Shakespeare's England," *The Elizabethan Theatre,* Vol. 7, pp. 134-55, 1979.

KANTAK, V. Y. "An Approach to Shakespearean Comedy," *Shakespeare Survey,* Vol. 22, pp. 7-14, 1974.

KNIGHT, G. WILSON. *The Wheel of Fire*. London: Oxford University Press, 1930.

LEAVIS, F. R. *The Common Pursuit*. Hardmonsworth, Middlesex: Penguin Books, Ltd., 1963.

LERNER, L. *The Uses of Nostalgia*. Schocken, 1972.

SEWELL, ARTHUR. *Character and Society in Shakespeare*. Oxford: Clarendon Press, 1951.

SMITH, JAMES. *Shakespearean and Other Essays*. Cambridge, 1974.

WEISS, T. "Breath of Clowns and Kings," *Nation*, Aug. 16, 1971.

NOTES

NOTES

NOTES